SHADE 2006

# SHADE 2006

edited by david dodd lee

Four Way Books
New York City

Distributed by
University Press of New England
Hanover and London

Editorial Office
Four Way Books
POB 535, Village Station
New York, NY 10014
www.fourwaybooks.com

Library of Congress Catalogue Card Number: 2004101060

ISBN 1-884800-58-0

The publisher and editor wish to thank Marianne Swierenga for her assistance.

Cover photograph: Nancy Mitchell. By permission of the photographer.

Book cover design: Cubanica

This book is manufactured in the United States of America and printed on acid-free paper.

Four Way Books is a not-for-profit literary press. We are grateful for the assistance we receive from individual donors, government arts agencies and private foundations.

This publication is made possible with public funds from the New York State Council on the Arts, a state agency.

Distributed by University Press of New England
One Court Street, Lebanon, NH 03766

We are a proud member of the Council of Literary Magazines and Presses

# CONTENTS

## JOE WENDEROTH (POETRY)

## JENNIFER WILLOUGHBY (POETRY)

## JIM ZOLA (POETRY)

## Raphael, Angel Sent by God to Heal a Sick Man, Stops Off at a Diner for Eggs and Bacon and Falls in Love with the Waitress Who Resembles his High School Girlfriend

*for Christian Andrews, for his 30th Birthday*

Tonight we wreck a bike, croon to the sky,
Wipe our pale hands on our jeans, palms glowing like wet jars,
Tonight the antique dew clings to our bellies. Dew on our
    feverish hands.

Tonight my brother speaks to me through the screen,
A green breeze, a telephone call at night.
He's tall and quiet and he won't come home anymore.

Tonight dead mice keep dropping like blood from
The fresh-cut cords of wood, the mice slow in the cold, tonight
The mice not fast enough the train coming.

Tonight we found a leak in the box,
The corner is shiny and dark. There's no doubt any longer
About the hex.

(The first night we drank from noon on and
My brother was willing to fight me for the fold-out
And I was not willing. The next night I wheedled
My way under the covers: one law broken, thus
Every law broken, thus every night ruined always,
As at night, when the seeds reach their fingers down under the
    light, under the earth,
Searching for something to hold and if I wasn't dead
I would hope they'd find something to hold.)

Tonight, vainglory like
A ballerina on a downdraft, mesmerized and slurring. Tonight
The curtain drops, paving the way
For a monster, the kind with parted hair.

Tonight I wrote a letter to the radio station
To enter the contest, the one where they're raffling off
A cardiac arrest.

Tonight I wrote your name on my hand and it appeared
In the sky. *Nice try*, said my old man, *but
That's not gonna pay the bills.*

Tonight I wish my feelings worked
Like in a bluegrass song, all sincerity and grief, only
The whiskey and blood daring to mingle.

Tonight, fear of the blue pen, tonight already been chewed,
Tonight, not our last, not mine, not yours,
Tonight, the radiator, the lamp by the bed . . . I know it's not
Life, but there's a heckuva resemblance.

Tonight a microphone stand like a wrecked bike in the living
    room.
Tonight a microphone in the bathroom, another in the kitchen.
    Tonight
I'm on stage, but in a sense
We're all on stage, always, and who isn't
Absolutely dreading the playback?

Tonight, if I ever should
Disappear, said my friend. Tonight, lend me your ear,
Said another. Tonight I don't care what's behind
The door, I just want the door!

Last night: left for dead in a tent with the rain
Coming down in flannel sheets, migrating to
The corners. But tonight? I'm adjusting—not pretending that I
    can come back
Because you can't ever come back, you can only arrive

Again for the first time. Because sooner or later
The schedule gets changed, someone else gets the plum shifts,
And the plum sauce is the real reason to get the Moo Shu
        vegetables.

Tonight, and every night, Tiger Noodles is the best Chinese
Restaurant in the world. But it's not in the world,
It's in New Jersey.

Tonight the telephone breaks another heart,
Tonight, "How Can You Possibly Be Happy without Me?"
Tonight, every man a penny.

# Why Can't You Remember My Name?

I just know I'll look back someday and finally
grasp what they call beauty, but for now I can feel
myself pedaling past it, out into some yellowed
and shorn cornfield, hugging the flat dirt, bawling
for it back. As for now I'm not impressed.  Blue

book. That dress is nice, I mean beautiful, I mean
on fire. In bed. With my wife. Reciting lines from
a screenplay we found in a coffee can, exploded,
then mending itself (but not properly), barren, damp,
scattered with every breath. The jack collapses leaving
the husband crushed beneath. The wife cracks three

vertebrae lifting the car from his chest, but what's love
without a body being broken? Hmmm??? The sound
carries better when the air is wet, but it feels early
in the movie and I hope I'm one of the leads,
I don't want to be dead yet. Drinking
from a fire hose. Fired from the chicken house.
My brother, all heart to stand up for me
but he was passed out drunk, swung in all the incorrect

directions, in retrospect it was my fault anyway.
Pull over here. The word of the Lord is right and true.
Obligatory guitar solo, but it's a pretty nice guitar solo.
My wife calls, she says, Honey, roll up your pant legs
before you leave. And I says, Honey, there's already

black grease all over, my cuffs shredded
like a gloriously-spent firecracker. The wind
an impenetrable defender. I coast off into the disobedient
weeds to take a leak and come face to face
with one of those little shrines that teenagers
erect when one of their kind gets killed in a car wreck.
Answering machine and all that. One whole week

where someone takes over like a dictator,
but a benevolent dictator. But heck, you'd have been
happy either way.  But then it was all over—
But what a week it was! Catching my mom and dad in the act,
then two days later finding out my dad wore a toupee.
Barstool—Stupid barstool.  The wide, surly clouds
spread out over the sky as if to dry,

as if everyone was waiting for me to speak. As far as I know
he never knew that I knew, which made it bearable
for both of us. Thinking back on it now
I'm crying again: how was it I never knew?

# Excerpts from *A Black Creek*

Last summer, at twilight time,
Before we went down to July—
As we drank, as the garden of the sea
As an invitation from broken glass, as
A touching tribute to Joe's late wife.
Tonight, like other times in his life,
He was in agreement. Broken stern.
Sarah on 3rd Avenue. Food becomes
A blouse, waving old ladies
Blue in bright-colored aprons.
In the intensive care unit with Anne Marie,
In what garden, by the levee
When giants fell by chance
By a solar eclipse. I spy voices. I spy the afterglow.
I spy barnacles just before
A night of fishing.

This is a wake-up call to kittens everywhere!
I am a modern poet! I am a plateau
Moment! I found Bird Song #111. I blew
Smoke at the cormorants. If heaven were
An ocean I'd pray for all the unmatched
Thorns. But life must continue (defective star).

[note: insert *the same blouse moves, the old ladies / wavelike, still
steel / blue on their bright colored shields*]

Afterbirth. Vainglory. First there's
A ballerina, soon after comes fear
On a mesmerized downdraft. She tried
To steal a segment of his life. He said,
"Not readily in the Hundredth," chinstrap
Wagging in the faulty sun. The curtain
Falls once again, paving the way
For a monster. And so, and so.
A real one. The kind
With parted hair.

## Tenting

*Scovill Point, Isle Royal, 1904: after a photograph*

It is a bivouac of women
in placketed shirtwaists and full skirts at ankle-length,
hair up in pins, each
perched on the downed birch log,
hands folded respectfully.
Father sits behind them, a little blurry:
the old juridical owl, in post-bellum whiskers,
giving the photographer his "summon the bailiff" look.
He wants his coffee,
and you can see it there, at the photo's center,
the little vessel of tin ware
on top of the cook pans and crates of supplies.
Who'll light the fire? Who'll take care of him?
The women think of their freedom
under the dining fly.
The lake wind ruffles the thick folds of their skirts.
The forest is a house without walls.

# Scheduled Stop

*from an early photograph of Isle Royale*

Ice-block and sawdust breathe the vapor of winter
on crates of gutted lake trout bound for Chicago
with northern tinfoil caught in their wide-open eyes.
Having just loaded them, three fishermen in coveralls
lean on the pilings, knitting their sabbath.
The steamship's prow is an axe of cream,
a sheet of foolscap on which is painted
the word: AMERICA. Under coal-smoke it comes,
under the black top hat: it is the delicate iron of civilization.
Fifteen feet up, at the railing, the tourists
in neckties and sport coats—gawkers,
readers of Ruskin or Walden, the
women in mutton sleeves and exogamous hats
look down on the wilderness. The
island's fir-tipped war bonnet
bristles like a painted backdrop.

# Inventory

I have no interest in knots
or the surgeon's selection of hoots—
I have only the mild curiosity of a tourist

when the fish's body is opened—
I'm amazed at all that purity,
pale bones and white flesh.

I prefer the calm
of an inland lake
with its inverted postcards,

or a teenage river, flexing its green arm
under the awning of trees
to the sea's open target.

Those gift shops
with their blown-glass seagulls
and china lighthouses give me the creeps.

What draws me to you is not personal or sentimental
or perhaps even human—
it is the Kantian angel

in me that wants to gorge on glittering light
and long horizon, until
the eye rediscovers its origins,

in the mirror of the absent self.

# Proto

Certain stones are older than all records
from a time before thumbprints or bacteria,
when the earth was someplace really quiet,

all angels and no television.
Thousands of years went by, and no one counted them,
the annals of fire and steam

before protozoa, before the airplane,
before the poet
whose bones feel they are eternal

but whose flesh knows he is grass and
ripe for the mower:
where he's going predates them, and the moon.

Scout around the bays. Each has been scraped clean
with the shoulder blade of an ox.
The continent sheds its sediment

and becomes the wreck that dreams are made of:
the lake approves it. All that blue in motion.
The mirror flashes in the wave's cup.

## Throwing Bones

Ben has the double twelve, the spinner, so he goes first. He puts it down in the center of the table with a sharp clack and a flourish. You look at the glassy edges of the spinner—picture-perfect twelve dots and twelve dots not just marked on the face of the domino but pressed into the plastic, little perfect dimples filled with black paint, separated by a little grooved line—and you think you can see his oily fingerprints on its edges.

It is your turn. There is cawing from the birds overhead and the wooden glugging of something in the water butting against the dock. It is a sound that doesn't draw attention to itself, but seems to serve a larger purpose, to point out how quiet it actually is, the way a picture of the watery horizon looks benign and miniature until you spot the little sailboat in the center of it. Your rectangular pieces are arranged on the table to face you. You scan them for one that has twelve dots. You find one and slide it, face up, across the table so the head of it touches the middle line of the spinner. You remove your hand quickly, wipe the palm of it on your waist apron, rest it momentarily on the living form that is growing beneath.

He is holding a piece in his hand, running one pale thumb slowly up and down the wide, enameled back of it. He does this smooth familiar curlicue over the edge of the piece with his thumb, and then slides it back down the unflawed surface of the front, over the dots that you can't see but know are there. His eyes are shut and you wonder if he is counting the dots with his thumb or thinking about something else.

"Go," you say. "We've got to get back to work."

"I am," he says.

You watch over his shoulder as a far-away sea gull disappears down into the chalky blue-gray of the water.

He puts the piece in his hand on the table face down, slides it into position on the other side of the spinner, and then turns it over. Then he smiles and you notice for the billionth time how his three teeth in front, the two big square ones and one of the pointy ones, all overlap one another at the edges. On the table the dominoes make a shape like a plus sign, or a cross.

You can play off the two he put down, or the four from your last turn. You look at the dominoes spread out on the table face down like so many tiny headstones, and then down at the row that is facing you and you find a two to play. He is the first to have to draw from the pile. He holds his hand out over the pieces and lets it float there for a moment before he descends. You stare at the thick ropes of blue veins that rest just under the surface of his white skin. You think how his skin must have grown to accommodate the blue growing underneath, and you are, for an instant, reassured. It is possible, then. You will stretch, too. And grow.

One of the men comes up the rocky slope from the water with his plastic apron on. He pauses on the other side of the ratty rope railing that edges the dock. He squints down at your game as he reaches behind him to untie the knot of his apron. "Who's winning?" the man says. You look across the table to Ben and he looks at you and the air is heavy with the smell of fish and blood that the man has brought with him, and then you say, "We don't know yet."

You look back up at the man and notice there's a thin line of blood, fish blood, that crosses his neck in a pale wipe from ear to ear, just under his chin. "You can't go in the restaurant like that," you say. "Not in the front door."

"Easy, kiddo," the man says, laughing. "I know that." Then he stops talking to you and says to Ben like you can't hear him, "You got a handful there, son. You better let her win or she might not agree to marry you." The man looks at you again, winks, and it's like he's projecting the most offensive edge of his scent right at you. "And then you can say goodbye to your job in her daddy's shiny restaurant," he goes on, lighting a cigarette, offering one to Ben. "And that fancy necktie, too," he says extending one leathery fishy finger to the bobbing lump in Ben's blue-white neck.

"We're not—" Ben says, dropping his domino on the table and holding his hands palm-out in front of him. "We're not smoking," he says, quietly. "Not today."

"Well, that happens," the man says, "they take away your necktie, you come see us down there. We'll put you to work."

And he points to the shed by the water, the bloodbrown one sort of tucked up under the dock.

When the man has gone, Ben looks at the shed and then down at his necktie, proudly straightening it so the knot is puckered just right and the wide arrowed end of it sits square in his lap.

After the man neither of you remembers whose turn it was, and you are suddenly and familiarly sick. With your forearm you push your neat row of dominoes into the center of the table where they fall, some face-up and some face-down, into the pile. Ben picks them up one by one as they fall and stands them on their ends, until all the dominoes are upended on the table: a curling parade of evenly-spaced dominoes that hugs the arc of the table and spirals into the center.

You and Ben look at one another until your time is up and then you both return to the restaurant, where you throw up in the bathroom.

The last customer of the night is a woman who eats alone: a powdery, breezy woman in a knee length polka-dot skirt that could be construed as frumpy if you didn't see the smooth white calves that extended from it, if you didn't see how those calves terminated in slim white feet strapped into very high-heeled patent leather sandals. Being her waitress, you see close up how her sueded cheeks seem to run straight into her wide, thick-lashed eyes, without dipping into hollows of loose bruisy skin like yours do. Her eyes are like opalescent stickers, stuck to her face.

You take special notice of her drink order, and special notice of the fact that when Ben makes it, he makes it very strong and plops two maraschino cherries into it.

When the woman leaves, you sit at the table she was sitting at, soaking up her bottled smell, as you wrap knives and forks and spoons in white napkins, sliding a tight paper collar around each one and stacking them.

Ben wipes down the jeweled bottles behind the bar. Twice you catch him straightening his necktie in the mirrored paneling. When you are both done you walk out onto the dock together. You stand by the table where your dominoes are still standing in a tight, spiraling row. "Hey," Ben says, squeezing your hand. "Let's go down there again." He points to the dark shed by the water.

"Why?" you ask, and then you say, "It's too late." Ben grins, misses your meaning, and says, "It's only nine." You explain, but he can't hear you because he has already straddled and crossed the ragged rope and he's starting down the stony slope, toes pointed in, leaving herringbone tracks in the mud. You push one fingertip to the domino in the center and watch as they fall in succession, a steady chain of falling, clacking plastic pieces. Then you follow.

The shed stinks of fish. It is dark and small, furnished with buckets and long smooth tables. Knives and other severe tools hang from the walls, glint in the light that comes from the high windows. The smell is made worse by the smell of cleaner—strong, industrial, no-nonsense cleaner—that mixes with it. It is a swirling organic-synthetic-natural-chemical smell that surrounds you. You run one hand over the flawless surface of the high rectangular table.

Ben is talking. He is loosening his necktie. When he has it off he holds it up close and considers it. "I think I'm definitely the kind of guy who wears a tie to work," he says.

His last sentence is louder; it comes from right behind your ear. Ben is behind you, reaching around you, working his thin fingers over the mother-of-pearl buttons of your shirt. And then:

Your clothes fall off your frame and you are bare. Ben has the heels of his hands over the jutting landscape of your hipbones, and you know that it is his bare body that is the furnace behind you.

You are sick from the smell and from knowing that if he moves a single fiber of his body, if he comes closer or steps away you will not be able to stand it. He moves his hands on you like he can, in such a way that inspires your muscles to a lazy languorous cat-stretch.

You reach your arms high above your head and then bend them back, your hands tracing the shape of his face. You feel with your thumbs how his eyes are set into his face as one of his hands traces the hollow around your belly button. You wonder if he can feel what is inside, if what is inside can feel him.

"Marry me," you say suddenly, before you know you're saying it. And then: "I mean it." You don't turn to look at Ben, but you feel the air and the blood leave him. He deflates, but he doesn't step away. He stands behind you, close. His knees lock into yours, his torso mirrors yours in the way it looks silver in the half-light, the way it gleams with sweat and salt and no-hair. You feel Ben's eyes scanning the fishhouse as his fingers play at the fine, flexible cloth your skin is.

"Marry me," you say again, louder, knowing that there is one thing he could say that would stand out like a slash of fluorescent yellow or pink across the bubble of muted salty sandy air between you, so that you think that you could see it, actually *see* his voice as it cuts a silver line that starts from behind your ears and then moves lengthwise down your belly and opens you and takes out everything that's inside, everything that matters, every part of you that's alive.

So you sway together, tall and thin and naked and six inches between you. You are shining square whitepale bodies, as yet unmarked and unruined but punctuated with dark hollows, waiting: to see who says what and which way you will fall.

## Ocean

This vast unbroken pool spills over our skins, falls still, and will
  not rage.
As we try to gauge depth, God, still deep, almost talks; the
  swimmers slither on and glide.

We remember as we often remember, we enumerate the reasons
  for being here:
the cold Vermeerian color, the blood on our ankles, the flavor of
  salt,

the hidden parting, the cold brine pouring over our cuts, the
  children playing,
the fact of what has happened, kneading and balling the wet, dead
  thought.

The small and varied abrasions bleed down, and in descent we
  see, finally,
our united states spread sleepily among us, hulking, hovering and
  nearly ready.

As we tread soundlessly over the icy miles, lovelessly, the black
  sounds come,
the memory of blood and our intentions as the waves come and
  come and come.

# St. Dymphna

*who intercedes for the possessed and insane*

We think of comfort as constructed simply,
an architecture of altar and tabernacle,
the place to hope for disasters when able
to engage in instinct beyond our decisions
we chose or didn't choose, an illness
we didn't avoid by standing in the rain—
the droplets tracing our necks and elbows,
attempting the artificial and sane,
the plain way of being able to resume
the graceless station of staying intent
on the natural impulse and its aching.
Hear us Dymphna as we become possessed
and stilled by all we would invent by being
icy, incoherent and completely content.

# St. Maria-Goretti

*who prayed for death instead of rape*

He turned his face away and hid, hid
in the darkest shadows of my face,
subverted the impulse to be mercy
and forced belief you wouldn't be missed,
clothed you in the raiment of his kisses.
He prayed but did not imagine hell.
I find myself inside the human race:
a constant sound to which my heart responds,
is not fond of, the craft that has contained
your frame of youth, your return to me,
your forgiveness and my concession.
Maria, pray for me now, for a reverence
I would have you understand:
my sincerest love, my simplest shame.

## Closet of Desserts

Anyone can steal anyone's dessert
Just by thinking of it,
And no one's the wiser.

Our dessert's substance is immutable.
Call it Floating Island of Release, The Debutante's
White Glove, Angel Panting at the Gate—it doesn't matter.

Folded into our dessert, reality and appearance
Can't tell themselves apart.  Non-existent, the split
Between subject and object, I and thou, being and nothingness,
Jean-Paul Sartre and John Stuart Mill, tractor and trailer, oyster
And pearl.

We speak of it often as we sit by the crackling fire
Which sometimes consumes a sofa
Or coffee table before we can stop it:
How different, without dessert,
Our lives might have been.

# Disabled Power Steering

1) YOUR DUDS
   Are *some* duds, I spent menopause
   Thinking.  Then gave my dog a sponge bath
   Out of sheer laziness, gave cussedness
   A shove, and some thought to

2) WAITRESS CAPS
   Which have transmigrated (samsara, I think)
   To taxi roofs.  BUT what happened to

3) TWENTY-ONE SHRIMP-IN-A-BASKET?
   No more do shrimp regularly achieve
   Their majority, leastways not here, where I was led
   By a true impression—a most hazy one—of

4) CAVES HAUNTED BY WHINING BRIDES.

5) IN MY SEASONAL WINDOW
   Just thinking makes me laugh, though
   I'm far from Chinese and my glittering eyes aren't gray
   But bilateral.  My symmetry is just about shot.
   I am still glad THE GREAT SURGEON's proclamation
   Lasted my mother till the end.

6) Maybe we'd like some place to chauffeur
   Our lives, or at least chafe them
   Over fresh Sterno, let the flames make us grin like early trucks
   Till night listens, and all together
   The ligatures tighten.

# Inadequacy

Some days you think you could be
Anyone's love, others you conceal your head
Out of shyness and wonder what unpleasant truths
Are steadily closing on you. You hope that a railroad
Will appear to supply you with good qualities.

It helps to keep principles in mind:
From the legs, technique. From the arms, expression.
From logs, wisdom. From twigs, impulses.
Then several items you've forgotten
Stare you in the face

And you have eternal questions, such as
Why grass seems to grow so well
Around trees and poles, and how do the branches of a particular tree
Give each other room.

Maybe this won't matter once you join the darkness
And mystery of the procession.

# Once

Once I thought that college would bring a glamorous social whirl,
Not a manual typewriter and a rubber plant
Acquired via coupon from the Lipton Tea Company.

Once I found a young man
In my swimming pool, but realized I had been
Poorly prepared for frolic.

Once I visited the Petrified Forest
And was mightily interested by the trees'
Iron stillness. The strange way they left me.

## *Someone's Been Taking My Books!*

Hearing this declaration from my own mouth as I wander through the chaos that is my de-alphabetized classroom library, I instantly know how my mind will someday go: slowly at first, in a low-grade paranoia, then ever more rapidly until I've achieved a mania comparable to that of Christopher Jacob Samuels, missionary, who during his ministry to the residents of upstate South Carolina during the first wave of the Great Awakening, became progressively deranged, imagining that his converts were pilfering volumes from his prized ornithology texts. In the end, he set fire to his entire library & devoured its ashes, thus sealing all those gilded wings inside him. However, appearances to the contrary, it's been proven that text comprises less than five percent of the average page; therefore, what Christopher Jacob Samuels consumed was mostly empty space, not only between lines & paragraphs, but within the deep wells of those minutely yawning o's & q's, the infinitesimal voids between ink fibers.[1] Also, there was the space separating individual feather barbs, as well as the hollows inside those terrifyingly light bones. Having taken in all that emptiness, was he then, when they buried him, larger on the inside than on the outside? I wouldn't know; I've never eaten a book; on the contrary, in fact, my books seem to continually move away from me into an ever-expanding universe of missing texts.

I'd like to believe that this perpetual migration is caused by students' petty larcenies or the books' innate wanderlust, each volume

---

1 Biblically speaking, of course, Samuels was merely part of a long tradition of book-ingesters such as Ezekiel, who was commanded to eat something the King James version identifies simply as "a roll of a book," perhaps some kind of scroll, which, though inscribed "both within & without" with "lamentations, mourning, & woe," tasted like "honey for sweetness"—also, John of Patmos, who was given an actual "little book" which also tasted like honey but instantly "turned bitter in his belly." There is no surviving record as to the flavor of the ornithology books.

possessing an itinerary on which my shelf is but one stop (*If you love something, let it go,* etc.), but the truth is that all of my reading life, I've been guilty of grave and premeditated transgressions against my books which have caused them to flee singly or in small groups into the care of others far worthier than me.

For instance, I confess to the felony of skimming; my writing students claim that watching my gaze flick back & forth over lines of print gives them the cold creeps, it's like viewing a process that can scarcely be considered human. *How can you read so fast?* they ask me. I'm not sure how I do it.[2] It seems the information is leaping out at me, but in fact, my technique probably involves some kind of mental suction—not, however, of individual words or sentences, but rather, of thoughts, images, configurations, associations, matrices, paradigms, archetypes, & ethereal essences. So what if the author agonized over intricacies of phrasing, penning each line with fresh blood, self-extracted in solitary confinement? As the logging company is to the sacred redwood forest, so am I to the printed word—on the outside, an unremarkable middle-aged teacher holding a library book; on the inside, Jabba the Hut, ravening.

Frankly, I'm amazed there's any print left on a page by the time I'm ready to turn it, which is generally less than thirty seconds.[3]

---

2. Though reading feels effortless while I'm engaged in it, not infrequently, I have to take a nap after I'm done. That's why bed is the best place to read. Ideally, it should be snowing outside—huge plump flakes that offer no hint of stopping or even slowing. In fact, my apartment door should be sealed shut by drifts, just as in Laura Ingalls Wilder's *Little House* series, the first real books I read on my own. Yes, & a wolf or two howling up at the Shell station on Rte. 25 or on the nearby Furman campus would be a cozy touch as well. But winters here in South Carolina are growing ever warmer, so instead of snow, I have yards of white lace at my windows; in the grayish evening light I can pretend there's a blizzard as I slip back & forth between the books piled around me & sleep, that other narrative.

3. In my own defense, I would like to point out that book time has never been the same as clock time; the fact that the books resent my reading them so quickly is clear evidence of a double standard on their part. Book time does whatever it damn well pleases. Unpredictable, inexplicable, it can clump up suddenly, only to elongate for years and then abruptly

Why do I skim? For the same reason I rarely read Henry James; if reading represents the intensification of experience, for me, skimming represents an intensification of reading itself. In ordinary life, moments are mostly filler, except for once in a long while when something significant occurs. In books, however, it's largely the reverse, though this is not true of the works of Henry James, that stutterer whose "amplifications, hesitations, and interpolated after-thoughts" distinguished not only his conversation but his prose as well, so that significance became inseparable from filler, and this was his genius, rendering him completely unskimmable, the very reason that on one occasion I made him fly—slogging through *Portrait of a Lady*, I found myself suffering such an agonizing mixture of admiration and frustration, I hurled the novel (Norton Edition with Selected Critical Texts) all the way across the room–the force, the trajectory as much a shock to James, no doubt, as to me, and possibly the closest he'd ever come to unadulterated physical rapture. But one enchanted moment does not a relationship make; my subsequent avoidance of his excruciatingly crafted prose proves that for all my avowed love of intensity, I am indeed a shallow skimmer whom books rightly long to escape.

As well as throwing books, there are other ways I have physically interacted with them that they must not have cared for. For instance, a forensic expert would not have to exhume my corpse in order to identify the contents of my final meal; most of the pages of my best-loved books are adorned with bright flecks of salad dressing and smears of spaghetti sauce–also, darker stains from coffee, both regular and decaf, though never with flavored syrup, Sweet N' Low, sugar, or cream. My books are not entirely dairy-product free, however; I used to read for slow hours while I nursed

---

snap back on itself. A book can take a lifetime to write, or it can tumble suddenly into the world, surprising everyone, not least its author who'd been merely doodling, playing around with an insignificant idea while relaxing between "real projects," when lo and behold, there the book is, raw and obstreperous as the newborn infant of that woman in the WEEKLY WORLD NEWS who swore up and down she hadn't even known she was pregnant–*Felt just like gas pains to me,* she remarked as the baby, cleaned and wrapped, was placed in her arms. *Come to think of it, I do recall being a little restless these last few months.*

my babies, who often temporarily disengaged to burp or cough, allowing the still-flowing milk to spurt out onto the pages. My books have suffered not only culinary degradation, but violence as well through frequent car accidents and disasters–in particular, the Spectacular Mazda Apocalypse of 1987 which merited the arrival of an entire battalion of fire trucks as the vehicle burned all the way down to its frame, sending aloft the smoke from library books that filled the trunk, including the complete works of Carl Jung as well as several scholarly interpretations of those works, each contradicting the others. I confess also to having ripped pages from weighty postgraduate texts in order to lighten my backpack; on crutches for an indefinite period of time, I rationalized to myself that this sacrilege represented nothing less than a survival tactic, as with my long-time hero Shackleton, who, preparing for the terrible march over ice after the breakup of *The Endurance*, tore from the ship's Bible the Twenty-Third Psalm and this (circumstantially redundant) passage from the Book of Job: *The waters are hard as with a stone, and the face of the deep is frozen.* The rest of the volume, which had been ceremonially presented by Queen Alexandra, he consigned to the ice. I imagine that the marks his men's cracked boots made as they turned away to begin the trek resembled bits of alphabet letters amputated from the language, then erased by blown snow before they could even set.[4]

---

4. Fire and ice–what is it about these contrary lights that so compels the imaginations of both reader and writer? In terms of Robert Frost's famous, bitter dichotomy, I prefer ice, whereas my writing students are clearly more drawn to fire. In their combined 287 years of life, they have sprayed butane into a TCBY parfait glass, and then, after adding a lit match plus water from the bathroom sink, snapped color photos as the sheets of flame flowed straight up the mirror; set a small grove of trees at the Greenville Zoo ablaze while roasting GI Joes with WD40; mixed white-out, cologne, M-80 powder, and lighter fluid all packed in modeling clay inside a racquet ball canister which they hurled at the football field's Astroturf. And it's not just the boys who love fire; it is the girls who mixed shoplifted samples of nail polish remover and Oscar de la Renta perfume to pour over the heads of their Joan of Arc Barbies. It is the girls who doused the blue synthetic manes of their My Little Ponies in kerosene and sent them soaring. It's the girls who slump in the back rows of darkened movie theatres sucking on cigarette lighters in order to exhale the fumes like blossoms of flame–inveterate readers, all of them, as I've always been. It's difficult, however, for me to remember

Then there's my lifelong habit of marking texts with underlinings so hasty they often run right through the words as if my intention is not to emphasize a passage but to cross it out, no doubt a symptom of passive-aggressive tendencies, especially in regard to the Bible, book of all my irreconcilable passions, whose margins swarm and blur dizzily with a violence of stars, arrows, question marks, exclamation marks, X's, private chronologies, and miniature maps and graphs. I do this with all my theological books; I've found their attrition rate to be particularly high, perhaps because they object to my scrawling such sentiments as NO NO NO by disturbing passages, though didn't Jesus Himself clearly claim that it's worse to be lukewarm than cold or hot? Thus, by the time I've finished reading and marking a book, it resembles the old graffiti'd women's restroom stalls in the Greenville Public Library and the Haywood Road Barnes & Noble, which were at one time famous for the ongoing debates between Wiccans, atheists, and fundamentalist Christians.[5]

---

how I felt at their age. I do recall it requiring all of my willpower to keep the cells of my body from flying apart or collapsing. No wonder I became petulant when adults accused me of possessing no self-discipline to speak of; I had neither exploded nor imploded–to demand anything more of me was nothing short of inhuman. Wasn't it obvious that I was exhausted from continually suppressing my powers? Weekends I spent at Spencer Gifts amidst the candles I dreamed of saving up for, in particular, the three-foot-long multiply wick'd old-time wax battleship manned with small wax vampire mannequins, also wick'd–no one who wanted it could afford it, and no one who could afford it ever wanted it. No doubt it still rests there, forever dry-docked behind glass. My *actual* life with fire, however, consisted of buying one or two candles a month. At home, they always seemed considerably less wondrous than they had at Spencer's with the neon lighting. Still, I'd sit with my candles in the mundane darkness of my room, dripping wax on the pages of Tolkien books, digging wax fingernails for myself, and daydreaming about torching the wax museum at Myrtle Beach (which I had never visited but loved to imagine), liberating such personages as Marie Antoinette and Elvis to melt, flow, liquefy into each other. Why did I finally abandon my fascination with fire? The older one gets, the more the mind longs to preserve distinctions rather than to dissolve boundaries. If you doubt me on this, just peruse the later poetry of William Wordsworth.

5 But the administrators of both institutions had them painted over–and at what cost to history? After all, what are bookstore and library

I also compulsively photocopy much of what I read; to a book, this must feel like the worst kind of soul theft, its essence burned away in a searing flash, transferred to a sheet or sheets of Georgia-Pacific Spectrum DP copy paper suitable for laser printers, copiers, plain paper fax machines, ink jet printers, and the majority of offset presses. While the book is suffering, I myself am undergoing a kind of powerful trance, as if I've been dreaming this dream since the birth of Gutenburg, pondering the seemingly autonomous waves of light released from the machine's inmost brain. I imagine that to anyone watching me, I must resemble

a.) a Dell-fantasy-paperback-cover-golden-haired-huge-eyed child leaning in to raise the lid of a bejeweled treasure chest from whose depth an eerie light is already illuminating his or her face

OR

b.) the flash-bleached 89-year-old version of myself, all skull in the flare's backwash. Either way, how could the process of photocopying be anything other than an ecstasy to me and a torment to the books?[6]

Yet in the end, this confession of my crimes against books proves to be, like most such confessions, vacuous. Just as the obsessive lover incessantly badgers the object of his devotion, demanding, *Why don't you love me?*, though not necessarily expecting an answer, of my books and of my reading life, I ask the same useless question, as well as others I find equally urgent, including but not limited to the following:

---

restroom walls if not the public forums of our time? Where else in the three-dimensional world are we to register our revelations and doctrinal upheavals? If a Martin Luther figure were to arise today in female form, how on these now-smooth metallic walls could she present the 95 Theses?

6 Yet this thought troubles me: Suppose that I could at last obtain an intricately-detailed, high-resolution duplicate of every beloved text, of the entire world, of even, perhaps, the universe itself? Where would I actually put it?

1.) Why does no one reward *me* for reading all the time, in the same way that commercial institutions regularly reward children by providing amenities such as a free Personal Pan Pizza Hut Pepperoni Pizza for every ten completed books? Am I not more deserving than some grease-guzzling brat who flips disdainfully through ten picture books just to get the damn coupon? Certainly, such a reward would put to rest my fears about the future of Social Security.

2.) Which of the following two Twilight Zone episodes most accurately represents my doomed obsession with books?

a.) the one in which the nerdy misanthropic bookworm, having fallen asleep reading in a bank vault, wakes to find that during his nap, the atom bomb has been detonated, making him the sole human being on the face of the earth. Rejoicing that he is now free to read without distractions or interruptions for the rest of his life, and exulting over the piles & piles of books that are now his alone, he stumbles & falls, his glasses slipping from his face & smashing amidst the rubble, leaving him *completely unable to read!*

OR

b.) the one in which doctors discover that a man suffering from unbearable headaches is actually the host of a rare parasitic insect which is boring its way through his skull. Enduring unparalleled torments as it completes its journey, & hysterically relieved as it at last emerges through (I believe) his right ear, he is horrified to learn that the torment is not over, will never be over: *the creature turns out to be a female that has deposited its eggs in his brain!* [7]

---

7. In a metaphorical sense, this happens the first time one hears even the simplest of stories, which is, of course, never "simply" itself, since it inevitably gives rise to fantasies, questions, interpretations, variations, & finally, of course, more stories—that full infestation from which there is no recovery. And as Greg Morgensen remarks in *God Is a Trauma*, "Reading can be traumatic...The trauma of one book supplies the subtext for another." (NOTE TO MY CHILDREN: Please have this statement engraved on my tombstone. Thank you.) Interestingly & perhaps paradoxically, the principle behind a cautionary tale seems to be one of *vicarious* trauma—that is, these characters suffer so that the reader will not have to do so.

3.) Annie Dillard states in her book-length speculative essay *For the Time Being* that the (human) dead outnumber the living by a ratio of 14:1, and that "we who are alive now make up about 6.8 percent of all people who have entered the world to date"—what are the correspondences in the realm of text, & how could they be calculated? And what, indeed, constitutes the actual death of a book—does its demise occur the last time someone reads it, or at the death of the last person who remembers even the faintest wisp of its plot? But what about the other texts it has (even slightly) influenced—do those keep the book alive, or merely seal it into a prolonged coma?

4.) Why does being a reader automatically render one a permanent weirdo-magnet? "That's a whole lot of books you've got there," comments the good-looking man exiting the library behind me. "You know, I recently read something that transformed my entire outlook on life."

"Oh really, what was it?" I inquire.

"*Mein Kampf*," he replies beatifically. "Would you care to discuss it with me sometime?"

5.) Well, why *shouldn't* one judge a book by its cover? Don't books possess information-loaded auras, just as certain psychics claim people do? Not once in my entire life, for instance, have I selected one of those drab-looking Penguin editions of anything, and I'm none the worse for it. Come to think of it, neither have I seen anybody else purchase one.

6.) Has a book ever been kidnapped, and if so, by what criteria was its ransom established? Why is the truest answer to the soul's loneliness an even wilder loneliness? Why in so many paintings of the Annunciation is Mary depicted with an open book? What *is* the relationship between the act of reading and the realm of angels? And why is it a documented fact that one of the most common human activities immediately preceding a ghostly visitation of any kind is reading?

7.) Who walked off with my only copy of Bill Olsen's *Vision of a Storm Cloud*, and why have you kept it since 1997? Was it for the poems themselves you stole it or for the gorgeously troubling photograph on the cover? Who has my big collection of Dianne Arbus photos of "freaks," and what does it mean to you in a personal sense? Which of your secrets are you seeking to treat? Are you keeping in mind that in the introduction, Arbus claims that freaks are the real aristocrats of life? Do you believe her? Have you ever been tempted to return the book to me, and if so, what inner resources did you have to summon up in order to resist? If I were to leave the classroom for ten minutes, would you find yourself able to replace it on the shelf?

8.) Is it actually possible to overstudy for life itself? If so, who determines the penalty?

The going. The letters. The staying.
The life of the little boy. The staying
and the life of the little boy. The
letter. The mushrooms. Dear Mom,
I'm writing to say how good it felt
when we took the mushrooms. Our skin.
The boy getting on the bus and the
street lamp. It's getting cooler. The life
of the little boy. The life of the little boy.
The going. The letters. It's getting cooler.
It's a little bit better. We took the
mushrooms and got on the crowded bus.
I'm writing to say how everyone seemed.

The wind brushed the cigarette
from the man's hand and the cigarette
drifted above the building and the fingers
burned and the air was hot or became
hot and the people wore their clothes
the way they wished to wear them,
and the office, and the brick, and the hand
that travels through the hair, and the hand
that travels through the ivy, and the
way he walked right there through the ivy.
The air is warm, the air is warmer, the air
is warm. He saw them. The people
were wearing their clothes the way
that they wished to wear them.

The world. I don't know. We sink. We
are awkward. We lean. We fall into doors
and we sink into those doors. The world.
I am dressed as one who leans into
one who is bigger than himself. The world.
I don't know. To be next to you dear
brother. I am positioned as the one
who leans into the one bigger than himself.
The world. The world. The party was horrible.
Falling out into the dark walkway or only
sinking into the evening. I don't know.
Doors are leaning up against other doors
and it is awkward. We sink. We lean. We are
as one leaned up next to one who is bigger.

The plane ascending. The beautiful clouds. The
light coming down. As in a movie you stood there
in the wind. The birds carried off. The ship
ablaze. The water lit. And smoke. The beautiful
clouds and the light coming through them. As in
a movie. The birds dip and flash their wings
and the wind. The sound. The beautiful woman.
And the beautiful wind. And the plane ascending
and the clouds. The light now coming down
in beautiful ways. Like a movie. I love you.
I love the way you do that with your hair.
The wind. The beautiful wind. The light. We're
all so smart. The plane ascending as in a movie.
Your beautiful lips as in a movie, the wind.

Someone's playing piano on the radio. The world.
The hot Americans. They're entering the building.
The world. The bell-shaped radio. The smiling
radio. Inside, the pianist thinks of the dark world,
of the people dreaming and of the people sleeping.
We've all learned. The world. The dark room.
The piano. The smiling radio and the stars.
The Americans exit the building. Themselves.
The stars. The dark night. The Americans playing
piano. The stars. The people. The buildings. The night.
I came to this country with a dream, and there was a
voice on the radio. The quiet and then the piano playing
again. The world. The stars. The people exiting
the building. The radio. The night. The Americans.

Perfect gray day above industry. The waterway.
The bridge with its opening and closing. The
practical turned mystical. The water.
The casting about. The stones. The grayness
illumines everything. The Buick and the light
upon the Buick. The plot, the dirt, the concrete.
Perfect gray day above industry.
The water. The light upon it. The parade.
The park. Across town. Light upon it.
The industry. The water. The grass patch.
A perfect day out there above the waterway.
The stones. The stones. The light across town.
The practical turned mystical. The industry.
Perfect gray day above an opening waterway.

The salt. The twin. The dilapidated morning.
Paul. Laura. There is some girl here with a
bitten chin. A little water on a wall of skin.
Do you care. The dog's bothering me.
The baby's bothering me. The sexy woman
got soaked, but I got soaked too, so what
does it matter. The salt. The twin. The dog
bothering me. The baby bothering me. How together.
How American. Paul. Laura. The dog's bothering
me. A wall of skin. A soaking waterfall.
Salt. The happy dilapidated morning. A shirt
on display in fashion's factory awaits you.
Do you care. The sexy woman soaked and unclothed.
Me, soaked. Paul. Laura. The dilapidated morning.

Drying off after an empty rain. Laura hiding outside town.
The sun coming out again. The wind and what the ancients
thought of wind. The sand and what the ancients thought
of sand. A warm day after an empty rain. Little waves
of the protected bay. And empty rain that never came.
The wind and what no one ever thought of the wind.
The brush and what no one ever thought of the brush.
The grass alive throughout the day. Tiny waves of the
protected bay. Laura hiding outside town. Wrapped together.
Wrapped together. First a thought and then another.
The sun doesn't need to bother. The wind doesn't need
to bother. Brush and grass. Wrapped together. The ancients
and their lonely existence. Little waves and wind's persistence.
Grass and brush. An empty rain. Ancients speaking out again.

## The Secret

*Prelude*

One life, one life, and so:
the secret life, it began so shyly,
glittering the highest branches,

breaking in droplets over rooftops,
a near mist, he thought, so quietly it came.
And though it seemed to fall

over everything, every gesture and scrap
of clothing, every word escaping
his lips, though it lengthened

its low green blades in the morning sun,
it lay forever at a distance
like music in a neighboring room:

*to split his life into two small lives, his*
*and the secret's, to divide the mind,*
*to break his death into two deaths now,*

*as if to multiply that one last breath*
*so that it might shatter into two breaths,*
*and four, a whole flock of breaths,*

*to bury himself in the living choir.*

1.

There are men, he thought, who grip
the secret so hard it shrinks
to the size of a fist, incarnate,

men who light his TV at dusk,
who lay their lives at the footstool
of the secret, unable to look up,

fierce with the shame that is their goodness.
Iconography flutters on a wall
like the papered shrine of a stalker's closet.

There are men who envy
the sweethearts of martyrs,
men whose death is the bride

of the secret, who slip into a ring
of wire, ribbed in explosives,
who cry out the way a lover cries,

in abandonment, in prayer.


2.

Though no one knows the truth
of the secret's birth, no one
would presume it had one

as we know it, there are tales—
like the story of the woman
downed in the booby-trapped jungle,

far from home, seeing
in her broken skin the arrival
of a force, the sheet gore

a glory, which, if not the secret,
is nevertheless its messenger,
the speed of the angel

come in a flash to fill the gap.
*God,* she said, cursing, *God* again
more softly now, like a call

to no one no one intended,
not fully, just the rising
apparition on her lips, a language

pouring from the open wound.


3.


Then he repeated the sweet syllable
in his mind, to draw back curtain
after curtain of the noise he lived in,

to let his body loosen its grip,
so that he might breathe in the air
of the secret, though it never came,

or if it did it came only as starlight
comes through a darkened window,
quiet as the hands of clocks

and thieves, as the ash that crowns
a tiny mountain of ash.
He looked through a book of songs:

*the Lord shall be thy shadow*
*upon thy right hand.*
*The sun shall not smite thee by day*

*nor the moon by night.*

4.

What would it take, he wondered,
to build a sanctuary for the secret,
to give it a home, a high roof,

since the secret was a lover
of ceilings that gasped,
of walls that coiled along the trim

like tiny scrolls of water
inhaled out of the seas.
That was the image of the secret

he conjured, having washed
at such an altar,
its glass rosette

a single mighty eye ahead.
Odd, he thought, the weight of caution
in this, our safe place,

our silver in the fountain;
odd, the rinse and shudder
of the prelude, a spirit

spooked from its cave of skin.


5.

*Here,* he said to his analyst,
*here is the child caught in rough surf,
the way the sea throws down*

*a shower of embers.
Here is the rusty sword in its spine
longing to slide from the rock*

*of the pelvis. Here the guilt*
*that charmed the sword.*
*Is it true, he asked,*

*we walk the extra mile*
*our fathers never walked.*
*Here are the shards of a day*

*I broke though I can't*
*remember how or when or if*
*it was me, as I was told.*

*I hold them up in the night*
*at my darkened bedside,*
*as if the gods, jealous*

*as is the way with gods,*
*might at last bend down*
*to steal them, to pluck the secret*

*fire right out of my hands.*


6.


Alone into the small hours
he sparked another cigarette,
its dart of smoke chasing the secret

down the impossible hole
in his throat as if to prick it,
to put the animal to sleep.

All night he lit them, losing count,
thrilled by the prospect of the next
last breath, the visual sigh

like a language in ruins: *feed me,*
going in, *feed me,* going out, and still
the secret burrowed, leading

with its lyre, slipping into the drift
of blood, as if it were enough,
this river of forgetting, the shush

of music dying into music.


7.

He had learned the art of smoke's abandon,
of meaning and not meaning,
opening and closing, of keeping,

as he reasoned, the heart aloft,
believing nothing, expecting nothing,
committing to nothing and not

committing; where everything was possible
the possible was nothing,
even heartbreak banished

from its clarity and sting
which in retrospect were nothing.
Too much irony will kill the secret.

Or too little. Too much of the upper
atmospheres, where the world is
a vertigo of words trading words,

cheap as kisses, and yet
a stubborn planet keeps pulling
at the mind until a mind can take it

no longer, and so lies down
inside the body, here
where the local myths begin,

where that sound you hear is a father's
shortened steps descending,
the dust and tangle of literal blood

like a net about the heart.


8.

The night the secret died he was out
walking the woods, their leafy shadows
eclipsing the stars, and the trees

which long had been the legs of the sky
were no longer legs, and the stones
sealed up their boxes of jewels,

and that flinching in the branches,
the first scant sparks of rain descending,
and nothing to do with fire and angels,

being no more, he thought, that *rain,*
though even this as he said it, the word
with its arms full of leaves, waking,

was just another sound among many,
just another wind to wander overhead,
desireless among its kind,

without a place to kneel or suffer.

## Cut of Dress

A woman in her fifties enters
the Brooklyn flat with her fee
in hand, two fifties as requested,
then sits at the white man's feet
in a chair, and closes her eyes,
believing while still in doubt,
and feels the draft of air pass
over her face—his breath? a fan?—
each time she repeats his words:
Breads are off my list, pasta
is off my plate, no beer (whoosh),
no wine (whoosh), no pastry of any kind,
not cannoli, silk pie, cream puffs,
tortes.  She feels no different
as she rises to leave, but in twenty days
she loses fifteen pounds, his face—
bored, lined, businesslike—
just behind her face in the mirror,
in the scale's reflecting plastic
shield above her pounds, set off
from her. She writes AMBROSIA
as girls might write their names
in copybooks in junior high where
she first became overweight, then fat,
then writes on the adjoining page
ABROSIA, one letter removed—
her first initial—and glues
the pages together, the word for fasting,
for wasting away on top of the food
of the gods, the folded egg whites
beaten stiff, the meringue folded in,
and the cream, and the drizzled rum.
At thirteen she was the May Queen,

she held the flowers in her arms
like a beauty queen or bride, but
she never married (*I'm too fat,
Am I as fat as she is?*) and never felt
as good as she does now, thirty pounds
by the 4<sup>th</sup> of July, enjoying the heat
of the room and the unairconditioned car
where she sweats and sings,
a hymn to loss and joy, for the past
being abraded, worn off, leaving just
stretch lines that she reads
as she might a news story, from top to bottom
of her body, from the left side to
the right, never enjoying her reading
as much as now in her diminishment,
the surplus value of her years of eating
given back to the air, her soul almost
inflamed again, on fire like Christ's again,
the desire strong again. Size ten
is a level of paradise, high humidity
a godsend, and if anything deters her
she need only return to the bored man,
feel the breath of inspiration, face
the mirror and the music, dance again,
hands above her head again, and rise up
lighter than air, into a man's arms
who must wait for this body, cleansed
and mined, a new-found-land, a slice
of life, fifty-two pounds lighter,
a fine piece, a find, a woman unveiled.

# Permanent Collection

If Rembrandt had dieted more and eaten lean, and perhaps only
white meat, then gelled his hair and shaved
his little mouse-face hairs, then had his colors done
—a bit more red, maybe auburn or rust—
instead of that dumpy brown, with a cork-colored wall behind him
—imagine it with flowers (hyacinths plus crocuses for *printemps*)
and he learned to smile—genuine too, not just for the camera
which was his eye, no, something to pierce you,
and he didn't have those belabored eyes, those sad-sack eyes,
imagine how he could get on in the world
we inhabit, where I for one look pretty good, alright, great—24/7—,
and if I didn't I'd call 911, or 999
at our London home, where we go to theatre almost biweekly,
seeing the best look their best, the buxom young ones who can
remember so many lines, and the measurements of that one—
83-60-92—who, it was said, "rose above the standard of perfection,"
oh metric world in which I perhaps would not fit.
And when I give my weight in stone, I feel so paltry,
nary-a-man, so narrow and contained,
I can barely say it—13 stone—
there it is. My unluck: my work-outs without stop have come
to that: 13 stone. But at home where bombs will be bombs,
I feel really good, I mean almost fantastic, with numbers that MAKE
SENSE, and not kilometers to go before I sleep etc.
Oh art world I love, your openings that open my eyes to this world
we see and without which we would not see quite so well,
how I enjoy you, and covet more EUROS with which to buy you
to make me more spiritual, more head over heels in love with
this LIFE. But let's not forget the REAL, the stuff that will fade
    and crumble
(I suppose it all will, come firestorm, come firebomb),
but Eva Maria Gonzalez, *la nueva* MISS ESPAÑA, what looks!
The way that sash
moves out and then in as if in a breeze, the fullness
of the S and E, and that inhale on the final ÑA,
and the pearls, the plucked brows and nose,
the deforestation of her underarms and French-cut

bikini line. Let's not go there. This is the place
to get off and disembark, alighting not in some foreign locale,
but a home of sorts, a thinking man's rest stop
with healthful options.

# Our Last Child's First Day of School

When we slip right into sleep, the way smooth
Like sheen from drink, we call that a nocturnal omission.
And when I slid right down from face to half-mast,
We said I was going down under, and this was Australia,
Equipped with kiwi hair, and this little island
A Zealand, old as the earth and eternal. But
Mostly we perform the paces of parenthood, moving
What was there back to back there, whether
It's some white doll that looks like trash, or the soiled
Undies that were flowery enough to wear for three days,
Or the pendulum movement of emptying the dishes
From sacred dishwasher, that diurnal tick-tock
That grates so. Everything is repetition, from
The snarl of disobedience, to eating the forbidden candy,
To the tormenting of one child by the other,
Until last week on our daughter's first day of school
We repaired to the room we're stripping
The paint off and caulking the cracks in,
And there amid the lucky ladder with spread legs just so,
The gentle hair of the paintbrush, and the lost
Power Puff Girl maze, we found our way back to bed
And what started this whole thing, that bending without pain,
That startling invention of fingernails, skin
Alert, interested in everything that's going on
And in, focused, one thing at a time,
And then everything at once.

# Clean

Even though my mother's mind is nearly gone,
if we give her wash to fold she likes to fold it—
with the pauses maybe it takes her an hour—
and then we take the pile to the other room
and toss it in the bag for her to fold again
tomorrow, or, perhaps, if she begins to shake,
later today, and she, a contented Sisyphus,
embraces the task, perhaps looks forward to it,
always a worker, always up to the challenge,
the undershirts examined for stains or tears
or loose threads that she'll pull and wrap around
her finger until the neck or sleeve almost
comes undone, and then she'll fold it,
sleeve to sleeve, bottom to top, as she's done
since life began, it seems. I don't disturb her work,
but when she is done, I ask this week's question,
believing as everyone tells you, that when
they are gone then the questions will come up
and wake you at night, that not knowing,
that knowing there's no one to call, and so
I ask, "Mom, did I make this up or did your mom
actually see Sitting Bull when he came to Manhattan?
I mean, did she line the street that day," and she
looks as if she's ready for the question and so
I embellish and pose it again, "When Buffalo Bill
brought Sitting Bull on tour to New York
was your mother down from the Bronx for the occasion,
in her mother's lap, or on a stoop swinging
from rail to rail, catching a glimpse
from the scalp up to that headdress, his skin
like a Puerto Rican's, a tomahawk in his raised hand
or the peace pipe chuffing away in his lips."
And she looks at me, her head a little bit sideways,
and doesn't say a thing. I remember my grandmother's
favorite phrase, *Can you imagine!*, and see them
all there, Annie Oakley with the six-shooter
to her head, Sitting Bull staring at Manhattan

the way he stares at gravestones, my grandmother
opening her purse for the streetcar or ferry ride,
and my mother is there on the sidewalk, giving
birth as usual, her head chloroformed, my father
in another borough, and when they hold me up
and cut through the cord with the tomahawk
she's out cold, doesn't say a word until she stirs,
looks me over, groggy from it all, and says,
"Don't talk nonsense. Whoever heard of such a thing."

## At the Museum

It takes vulnerability to display a sense of solubility. Well this poem is an attack on glow. The question is then to change her life with a yellow coupon. *Everything looks brighter than before.* No doubt damages will surface and contrast to guess a difference. *Lordy, don't leave me all by myself.* She does not know if God exists and breaks inside her. A great ghost lives in the subtlety of her flaking paint. *Peel my breast, corner me with brush strokes, slash the life off my cheeks.* The midwife declines the invitation to crack down on restoration. It is pointless. There's a bombshell slapped in the face of the sky. *Open up and see.* Her erotic soul seeps through savage strokes. *There is nothing left.* She is nailed to a wall and shivers under the brush of a breath.

# Step One

So it had to change. She stole (their) names and ran across hearts. She wanted an occasional sidewalk from cityscape to wilderness. Something had to change. Her mouth. Buried in flowers. There was no moonlight sonata. Please, don't get me wrong, she wore her lips naked before rolling into the American design. When her eyes looked for a foreign landscape they fell on an Afghan carpet blue with. She wanted her name like a brick under her feet. Something had to change. She smiled with a blue thread between her teeth. *I love the way you move.* She stared at her deaf like a picture. Gave her a song. Drove her into dust. She loved the way she moved. She wanted to wear her name. Loved the way they moved. Something had to change. Her feet kicked her eyes shut in this American design. Bruised like her mouth under a brick.

# Vibration in the Line

For a week now she has been troubled and her thighs are heavy with grief. The cat nibbles at her shoulder through the sleeve of a woof sweater when she sits with Malte Laurids Brigge in a cold bed. *A good intention but in some ways I don't think it gets any easier.* What if she pulled off these bulging veins before they spill on the white sheets. That she watches foreign movies for a week is a difficult thing to say when she came from abroad and the necessary spreading of surrealism on the screen scares her. She likes that the iron sits under the easel when she speaks to her about the future. *She looked words onto them, certain words that she needed and that weren't there.* And then there is another day. She wears a ruffled shirt and she wears a snazzy boa sweater and she does not know this word when both of them decide on black for the rest. *Les films étrangers ne sont pas étrangers à cette étrangère.* It is not always bright in the bedroom when a hearse is hauled around the Eiffel Tower by a camel.

## Mostly Ocean

I have tried to reach land,
over and over, holding

onto crags for map, but packs
of hounds chew their tongues

off, lined up like a row of
soldiers, waiting for my first step

onto rocks that bank like
forks. I am hardened by this

living everywhere. At last,
one day I make it onto beach.

When I am inspected, they
discover a likeness of lost,

barnacles of want. I ask:
What is likeness but a desire

*to build an empire?* I barely
make it through. As I look

back at the sea, I know my body
will always be mostly ocean,

a disease stitched into me.

## "She Was . . ."

(4)
being singled out by her swimming instructor
for her mastery of the lifesaving dive:
arms out
straight drop of the body into water
keeping the head afloat,
never going all the way under.

She couldn't do a regular dive
or hold breath long enough to swim
one lap of the pool.

But she could do this jump
over and over
with an instructor barking

Girls! Now watch her. It's perfect.


(1)
putting blood roses on a stone
and even though she was only a character in a country song
what she was doing made sense to everyone.
Nothing, not even Tennessee, could stop her from going
to the top of that abandoned hill everyday,
revisiting this man who was the other half of her insides.
Like the groove in her tooth
she sought with her tongue
when she was being driven around in taxicabs.
She could still hear him speaking—
Beautiful is easy
now she was remembering out loud.

(3)

working hard to convince everyone around her.

Yes, my father.

When I was 6, 11, 13.

She was creating a caste system.

Placing stones and pebbles in piles.

In far corners of the country
she pulled strings and took spas.
A facial didn't mean anything.
What meant something was attention.

Belief.


(2)

dancing at the strip club in a windowed box.
He used to come every Saturday night.
Even brought his wife one time, see how pretty she is?

He thought marriage would set all his fractures.
The Orpheus a balm in his split skin.

She kept dancing.
Wives no wives
it didn't make no difference
each move was still the same.

She thought the same thing when her boyfriend
broke in that night,
right before he pulled the trigger,

Here he goes again,

here he goes.

# Tyrant Spirit: Cantos

Canto 10

*Apocryphal Blues*

Unearthed, am I a chronic veteran spent
roadside, glimmering night-tide wind-swept ice
over form, ill-effect, percussive sweat
—idiot balance, overtured chaos,
left wing branched out white failure, tugged in blue?
I remember the view, so orange ago

freight train winding up my shoe like a move
without forgiveness. What of it? I'm stewed.

Canto 47

*Marxist Theory Provided*

Mustang fuse—corroborator daughter.
The future is a chair against the wall.
Strip the riddle. You can't get blurred for hur-
rying. It's how you leave a ghost not the crawl-
space. It's so much larger when you're armless
strapped inside the shade of North Begonia.

If you could break your brittle bend, undress
words from flesh, you'd come into love not death.

Canto 83

*Fall the Fall*

A deep depression's setting right across
us like a new intelligence—Give me
another horse!  Subdued, unarmed, I brought
a burning book to your embassy,
remarkably. Self-importance is good
enough as evil, the knowledge swift

as a greasy heart without a chest, look!
My brain's higher, wired in advance. Pluck.

## Hollywood Beach Idol

Every morning I stop for coffee and chat
with the lifeguards who are all addicted
to American Idol and have strong
feelings—one way or the other—
about Kelly. All but the Native lifeguard
with the radiant ponytail.
He was taken from his reservation
by the Canadian government
when he was just a baby and raised
by a white couple from Toronto
who often vacationed here
in Florida. After years of looking,
he's just found his birth mother and father,
still in Canada, and is saving to bring them
and the brothers and sisters he's just met
on a trip to the Hollywood Boardwalk.
He's above the nonsense
of American Idol, you can tell,
and once he's ordered his iced latté,
he's on his way to his hut with only
a smile and a nod. The other lifeguards
resent him, I think, for not sitting for a minute,
for not voting, for not having any curiosity at all
about the show. After the article about him
in the *Miami Herald*, complete with a picture
of the reunited family in Canada,
he's been contacted by producers
to sell the rights to his life story
for a TV movie. The lifeguards debate
who should play the lead *Lou
Diamond Phillips or Johnny Depp*.
"He'll have to watch that, won't he?"
a blond guard says, wiping his silver whistle

with a napkin, peering at his reflection.
"But wait a minute.
Who'll play the rest of us?"
We all laugh. The blond fluffs
his bangs. "You guys, I'm serious!"

# Hollywood Beach Pantoum

A smack of translucent jellyfish quiver
like silicone implants on the shore.
Tropical parrots squawk lime green gossip
in the palms. At daybreak, a porno flick

full of silicone implants
is being filmed at the Hollywood Beach Resort pool.
The porno director flicks open his palm pilot
and the actors eat soft-serve between takes.

Tourists buy film at the Hollywood Beach Resort
and snap their kiddies in the same pool
in which the actors ate soft-serve
a few hours earlier. One father

snaps his kiddies until the film's spool
is up. One mother invests in a henna tattoo
a few hours later. The father has to be
reassured it's a whim, nothing permanent.

One mother invests in a henna tattoo
as tropical parrots squawk lime green gossip.
A tattoo artist reassures her *nothing permanent*.
A smack of translucent jellyfish quiver.

# Casino

When my sister says there's been an accident, I think car, then bus, but she says no "escalator" and "pile up" and I picture the bodies, my mother on the bottom of fifteen casino-goers, her hair (a perm) caught in the moving steps *bump bump bump* against her back. Someone pulls the bodies off one by one and lifts my mother as though she is light as a dust mote. A man sits her on the dirty casino carpet, the top of my mother's head pulled away. Someone else puts my mother's purse in her lap, and my father, fifth in the pile up, finally finds my mother, sees her sitting there, like a shocked little girl. He tries to walk towards her, her bloody face, but faints, then crawls to her instead. My mother's eyes are as blank as tokens.

When my sister says the word "scalped," I think cowboys and Indians, tiny shrunken heads, the blood all boiled out, warpaths.

Yellow chips polka dot around my parents and the other people who've fallen on the escalator. Coupons for complimentary lunches. A few desperate passers-by pick up the free money instead of helping, quarters streaked with blood darkening their days.

My father curls like a cashew around my mother so she can lean into him. Workers circle both of my parents, to shield them from the stares of tourists out for a drink and a game of slots. My father's left hand is all cut up, his wedding band is shredded and sharp. He doesn't know yet about his heart, how he'll be hooked up to the monitors soon.

I remember my mother telling me to braid my hair before riding the Ferris wheel and a story about a girl's loose curls flying into the gears, being torn out in chunks, her blood, warm red specks, dripping onto the seats below. And how the carnie had to stop the ride with a jolt and how a fireman shot up in a bucket truck with a pair of scissors to release the screaming girl. When the ride went back on, the passengers got off, one by one, no one smiling or laughing anymore. And I was never sure if my mother was on that ride or in the park that day or if it was just a story she liked to tell. The girl's hair scattered, whipping by the horses in the Merry-Go-Round, twisting into the cotton candy.

And my mother's hair, also left behind in some gear, her blood soaking the silver escalator steps, the casino carpet.

Up and down and round and round. All the bald lemons and cherries spinning.

## Jarslov Irenczivic's Seven Habits of Highly Effective Foreign Intellectuals

**1. Take unexpected stands on hot-button issues.**
Globalization is something I consider thoroughly enchanting. Far from being in favor of grassroots, community-level organization, I think globalism doesn't go far enough. There should be one leader for the entire world—chosen randomly, obviously, as it would be impossible to agree on an election process. Every person in every country should wear the same uniform. Individualism is to be avoided—it brings pain, and besides, it's banal. The only people who should be allowed to be individuals are Hollywood stars. They've earned the right. Especially that Joshua someone who plays Pacey on Dawson's Creek. To me, he's the <I>image</I> of the solidly grounded, emotionally honest person and that's significant <I>on its own</I> – I don't believe there's anything illusory about it. Media creations are the most honest figures in our culture. Unmediated people lack a certain brio.

**2. Use a mixture of historical references and pop-culture buzzwords until your audience is too confused to challenge a thing you say.**
Stalin bequeathed us some underrated methods for practical action, but as we saw in the film "The Sum of All Fears," binary oppositions have undermined the left since the death of Lenin. Hannah Arendt was only one answer—Jeaneane Garofolo is another. We won't be able to address imbalances in areas like the music industry, where Internet file-sharing threatens to undermine legitimate claims of artists such as Metallica (a group I admire) until we embrace a Socialist ethos. As we rewrite the globe under more unified terms, we can dispense with either/or totalitarianism and celebrate a kind of radical invisibility. The more attention we pay to the lives of Hollywood emblems of health and happiness like Brad and Jennifer, the easier it is to erase ourselves as individuals. Liberation will not be far behind.

**3. Seem to embrace things that are abhorrent. No one will know what you stand for.**

I love surveillance. I want more surveillance in the world. I don't want to be unwatched for any moment of the day! It's a thrill to know that someone is listening to me and watching me every minute. Personally, I love it. You know the security cameras in banks by the automatic teller machines? I would love to get that footage and edit it into feature-length films. People staring into their bank balances—the emotional costs of capitalism caught right there, on film! Shock, dismay, confusion, self-hatred—you'd see it all. The important thing is to observe, at all times, someone doing something, so that you don't have to read an interpretation of it. There's far too much interpretation in the world. I would a thousand times rather be a security guard than a university professor. It's a clean, unmediated way to make a living, and you get to carry a gun.

**4. Have at least one show-stopper of a theory, something no one can accept or stop talking about.**

This miraculous thing of having babies underwater should be extended to having societies underwater. Now you'll say to me, but Jarslov, the adult lung is not intended for breathing in water. And I know that's true, but with stem cell research the remarkable capacity of the human body to adapt is just beginning to be explored. Underwater societies are not so far-fetched as you suppose. And there are so many benefits. They would have more fluid boundaries, obviously, and less sectarianism. Warfare would be conducted very differently. And governance would not be as complicated because no one would be able to speak. It's a no-brainer. They'd work better than oxygenated societies.

**5. Throw out an exceptionally unpopular stance that cements your reputation as an independent thinker.**

I'm not in favor of women's rights. That issue has become a distraction from the fight for liberation. Women's rights are a chimera, something undefinable that will either be there or they won't—we can't fight directly for them. Women would do better to just be pleasant people throughout these difficult times—the results may be more positive for them, come the revolution.

## 6. Contradict, Reverse, Win.

As soon as you've said something as unpalatable as the statement in #5, make sure to reverse its effect by saying something in direct opposition. Such as, "Women are much smarter than men, and their powerlessness is a mystery to me." The contradiction will not annoy your listeners as much as the extreme prejudice of the earlier statement. The audience's need to feel sophisticated is not outweighed by their need to feel good. Americans are very childlike in that sense.

## 7. Leave 'em Laughing.

Always close with a joke. Something light, whimsical. Here's a good one: What do you get when you pour boiling water down a rabbit hole? Hot-cross bunny. That's a good, safe joke. You don't want to go back to difficult areas of your talk unless your audience leads you there. Even then, a lighthearted approach to their outraged questions is best.

## Destruction of Names

A poet's use of names is frequent
but in each naming is the sign of lost
faith. She forgets her subject, points
to appelations. The poor dead name
limps as if it knows.  The party was over

last night. Names are the marks of
luminosity gone wrong among plain
objects, with God lost. A name is a mystery
chopped. This is the poet
who loved dancing once.  She can

remember the powerful waltz
and the eros.  She would follow him
to his car, not bother to name what
they felt or did.  Found her lover's
hand, raised it to her breasts.  Now,

dislodged from the world of passion,
left to molder on the outskirts of her soul,
she has nothing to build on but naming
in her lonely poems, all pieces of her desire.
She has become a name.

Does naming kill the soul as it names?
Stop its flowing, the graceful slope
of a body in love? Can she descend again
to flowering worlds of all things glowing,
showing forth without names?

# View of the Twin Towers from Bleecker Street in the Village, 1974

They tower to the south, out the window.
Two weeks we stay, amazed, on Bleecker.
NYU seems happy, close by below.

We come to culture that July. Good
Friends lend us four rooms. So, seekers,
We see stalagmites. South out our bedroom window:

Tall towers. Night lights. We're awestruck. Though
They're stable, they sway. Cowered, weaker,
NYU appears happy to be close by. Below.

We learn the Big Apple, we think. But we're still callow
As we trade high NYC for low house, upstate. Peekers,
We peeked daily to the south. Out the window

Early each day. Finally, to one tower's top. I bellow,
"I have to get down!" You snap rivers. Meeker
(like NYU), I am content on the ground. Close by.

We worry about fire. But by plane? Highest hell—oh
Who could choose it? *Run down quickly* . . .
Towers to the South in our minds. Out that window
Like NYU, we are some who saw them. Close by. Below.

# Scars

Some second brother and his cancer death:
age twenty-seven. Your first wife—Jane.
The tricks of love are often like the pain
of your first son from his very first breath

seeming not to love you, throwing a stick
at you. He was two. Everyone is lame
from the pain of the past.  Hates it, will kick
against its pricks.  We all know the same

limp near the door of more and more sin,
loathe our Fibber and Molly Magee den
stacked with lead-like stuff. Not enough
time or will to clean. Not unrelated, rough-

ly similar:  Think of how at any new dawn
morning glories open and then they yawn,
as if throats could drink truth, beauty, all
twenty-four hours.  But we see how tall

and tight they shut in bowers each night,
sleep, wait, gain strength to greet great sun
again just one more. Will they again grin?
Like us, they know: each glow of bright

white light is still so terror-filled, stark,
it first fills, but thrusts down. Delves to dark.

# Event Journal

Enormous second in which the neighbor girl walks into the house
in a yellow shirt, saying Henry Henry because her mother wants to
    buy some eggs
or because the chickens are loose in the corn
In that second the silence around the afternoon sheared
Traffic on the highway returns
Perhaps it is a paradox
an arrow will keep traveling
a hotel will always be vacant
on Mt. Blanc
Who is most ravaged by the mother's death:
Cash, Jewell, or Dewey Dell
"What is the nature of each thing"
A second a fiction
of then, now—
a houseboat on stilts in the forest
a girl in a yellow shirt
One winter when the road stuck us all in our houses
the hotel for a minute slid off
the eggs froze in the barn
We went to sleep with snowdrifts
turning to horses or daughters or fish.

# Wisconsin

On the clearest day the gramophone fell from the wagon
The land filled with misdirection
Nowhere to go but through
I love you whispered the river
Will not leave you added the buzzard
The sky sank down like a citizen
We lived in a canyon in the Wasatch
a third-floor walk-up in Manhattan
Now the land in the middle contains me
for a small price as small as an onion.

# Questions for the Beloved at the Cow Pond

Swimming out I got wound up in weeds, the water dark
and green except the body parts it.

Which method
do you favor—which mosses, whose mouth? Cricket house,

motor boat, law? A lost set of keys
underwater, a drought?

# The Verb *To Plant*

*My words don't mean anything I know, they are just seeds,*
*if I eat them in a row they show me heaven.*
*— Eric Felderman*

*This word grew from the sole of your foot.*
First there is a plant, it is just the plant,
it is medicine. *An herb.*
Then it is planted.
*To place or set in the ground to grow.*
It is a gold pot in a tall office.
It is people coming to water the pots with buckets.
*To establish; "plant a colony."*
To planter. To bucket the gold.
The buckets are planters, filled with plants.
*"The entire plant of the university."*
To universe. The entire universe of the plant.
The plants do not live outside.
*To set firmly in position; fix.*
Is it really called "a plant"?
If it grows outside, is a tree a "plant"?
*Any of various organisms of the kingdom*
If tree is plant then human must be plant.
*Phantae. . . lacking the power*
Suddenly we are all planted
in the ground. *of locomotion.*
To flower. (Yes)
*The breath reveals an animus; if it is emphatic.*
I am becoming tree.
*A scheming trick; a swindle.*
My throat trunk, my head leafy branching.
*A person put into place in order to mislead*
*or function secretly, especially:*
The rest of me planted and everyone planted.

To medicine. I tree: we.
*Group of buildings for the manufacture of a product.*
Each person. Heads above the ground.
To human the plant. *"plant oysters"*
The heads like tombstones but still really heads.
The entire plan of the universe.
Everywhere there are people they are planted people.
*Anything that breathes.*
To kingdom the human.
Their bodies grow down, glowing white roots.
*To fix firmly in the mind; implant.*
Stretching wings through sleeves.
*To station for the purpose of spying or influencing behavior.*
Earth surrenders pathways to us becoming it.
We: often crowded.
Some cannot get sun.
*An action in a narrative that becomes important later.*
"To change all the way," she plant said.
(Rock-a my soul in the bosom)
Our faces contain sun place should enter.
But sun reduce to sunflower.
It spin like pinwheel.
*"planted a gun on the corpse to make the death*
Flower elongate
to funnel
pulse not blinding.
*look like suicide."*
Color which liquid wet not.
*Place in water or an underwater bed.*
We go, through. To through.
We planted not planted earth any longer.
(O rock-a my soul)
To human no longer the earth.
What our bodies disappear.
To were.
*"'The rite of revolution is planted in the heart of man.'"*
In drop we. Entirely to.
*The place so as to discover.*
And then, we everything.
*To deliver [a blow or punch].*

It spinning all black conclusion is.
"This," she said, "is what I'm talking about."
To become. Not becoming any to longer become.
*From Latin, "planta," sole of the foot.*

# Baby Shamanics for the New Millennium

Everybody's pregnant. I myself seem
not to be pregnant most of the time. When
I am, I dream the baby's in a shoebox.
We're all on a plane. The baby is blue
(but I don't think that means it's a boy).
In the morning mint rises up from me, a fleeing vapor
it flees, has fled. Mint. Blue mintine babies
abandon my lungs like tiny forest peoples
with tails and spears. I don't know where
they're going, they won't tell me.
They run themselves into a vortex
which tumbles off down the mouth
of an enormous fish.
Do they even know my name?
Can you see what I'm talking about?
I feel like a million luckless heaps of laundry,
all the mint blown out of me.
The basement is musty and mintless,
covered with coughs. Everybody
who's pregnant smokes too much
and must learn to take care of
the babies. Those babies are
blossoming like swirly lupine, their bright
bobbing beings appearing on earth
out of nowhere. First there is just us
in the room, then there's a baby.
Sucking and sucking.
So much of it seems to be wet: the becoming
of things, the letting go, the fleeing minions,
our love our eating our grief.
I am not yet ready to die.
All the onesies in the dryer
I've been saving for our beautiful blue somewhere.

# Affliction

*in which the shade...has come out of the grave to catch her....*
*[in which she has slipped] out of place or fastening*
                    —*Victor Turner (*The Ritual Process*)*

Yellow jackets enter the dizzy
phosphorus: a man with his medicine
chills the elegant wax, cures
the grass with a kiss. It's an ugly

truce, a neatness, a snapping,
this war for the safety of my garden.

We shuffle the tantrum, the common pink
day yanked from its mild hour.
The swarm of flustered drones—outcast
saviors—sway toward the vanishing world.

Somewhere a low song, beneath
crumbs, parasols, blood, spades: a splendid
roar unfurling in the blistered nether.

I have elected a silence with embers.
The papery orb breaks open. Cell
by cell the would-be assembly, her own
white womb, smolder and crack, expire.

Still somewhere she roosts, endures,
fiercely swells in the darkest chamber.
She purrs like a brain.

And I may never find her
and I may never know.

## Divination

If death is annihilation of time
then its equation is manageable.
I've come here to say
I no longer want figs for breakfast.
The earthy flesh stands for nothing.
Tastetreatiness is easiness disguised.
Besides the season is shifting
and with it, go I slowly, admittedly,
but on my way nonetheless.
We guess at meaning and meaninglessness.

Which god was it who chose to be stone?
*None*, you say. And I say, *Bullshit*.
It was the one who watched
as you lit feet first on fire
then hurled yourself into the river,
existential and extinguished all at once.
Okay, so it wasn't a god maybe
and perhaps it wasn't even you
but does it matter at this hour
who was the shooting star?

# Like This

The asbestos specialist's son
is on fire again. Like this

rule of human tomfoolery,
I know you have betrayed me.

You slide your middle finger
down the blue divide    of her arm

to her palm and you're there.
Where exactly you're not sure

but it doesn't matter anymore.
I'll ask of you the essential: water

to shorn root. Just tell me the truth.
It's here, the corrupt assembly

begins rising within me.
Like this    I want you to know

more than your words, I want
you to know what I know.

# Apology to What Remains

Orange smoke rises off the water,
a maple tree moves as dusk disguised.
Nothing is as it seems.
I wish my daughter was the rain
on the wooden steps. I call,
*Look! The moose
is heading for the island again.*
Her body holds the blue chill of water,
as she runs across the porch past me.

The turtle shell she found
lodged in rocks one summer
stirs on the mantle.
Apologies are never simple.

I remember the story of a famous surgeon
gone mad. During a meeting,
he looked up from his papers
then down at his two ties.
It was the eyes
of his colleagues that confused him.

I took my daughter's body
for my own in that same confusion
that has the clarity
of dressing for the morning.

I have searched her room for something
and found only hair from her brush
in the trash. It makes a small wreath
I keep pressed between my palms,
nesting material for birds with little mouths.

They fly through me through
the vacant joints of the turtle shell,
to the antlers that hang
above the mantle, their path
a constellation stringing us up.

# The Play

## The Setting

A beauty salon located in a mini-mall called Alpine Village located in some nameless city that is not too large and not too small, but just right. It is a growing city that has yet been untouched by population explosion, or brand new mini-malls, or graded hillsides of grass being readied for suburban blight. The salon is still called a beauty salon. It is not called anything funky or new that could be considered anything close to cool. It is not even retro cool. It has a glass front window, the salon chairs are not a funky blue or pink plastic, they are not seventies brown or green, they are not metallic or stainless steel. They are just nondescript chairs and non-descript sinks. There is a counter up front with a few newspapers stacked on one corner. There is no rack of perfect new products with cool names like Goop for hair or Paste for hair. There are no old products either that might have been sitting there since the early 60s, that some watcher of *The Antiques Road Show* might find a find. The salon is just what it is—a family business that is not pretty, not dirty, not cool or hip, but open, and people are getting their hair cut there because they need their hair cut.

## The Characters

**Dave Fenson:** He's a hair stylist—straight. Thirty years old, just a touch of gray in his hair at his temples, wears glasses from the late 70s, but still they look okay—not too nerdy. He's going through a divorce. His wife's name is Joan. She's into theater and singing. She's got a great singing voice. It's powerful. She also has a kind of a big nose. But Dave likes it. It's just that they don't really see eye to eye on things any more. She wants to have kids and he has already had a vasectomy, but she also wants to pursue her acting and singing career, and he's not getting in the way of that, so he doesn't understand why the divorce has to happen. He doesn't really talk to his customers about his divorce, though. He only mentions it if he thinks it will help them with whatever they are telling him about their lives. He's been married for five years.

**His mother Tina:** Reddish-blonde hair, it's a little thin at the temple. She still rats it on top to bring it up. She owns the beauty salon. She leases the stations to the beauticians. Her shop has always been in the mini-mall called Alpine Village, so all the buildings have an A-frame point to them. The wood on the shingles is dark brown. The people in the shop next to her own a pet store, but they don't sell pets—just pet food and pet products. The pets are too messy. Her son Dave likes to make stained glass windows as a hobby, so he made a large parrot out of stained glass and put one in their beauty salon window. The joke is that they have more pets than Pet Village. She likes to go skiing in the winter time and meet fellas in their fifties. She's sweet. She was married to Dave's father a long time ago, but he took off, so Tina lets Dave run the show—the shop.

**Joy:** An overweight stylist who works the station next to Dave's. She's needing to lose over fifty pounds. Breathes hard as she moves. Coughs from a cold she is trying to get over. Has to go out back for a cigarette on every break. Her hair is stylish, but it doesn't look good. It's burgundy some days or on others it's something else. No one is really sure anymore what her natural hair color was. Is trying to eat healthier, so she has a brown bag inside a plastic Safeway bag and in it is a large bag of trail mix, some yogurt that she keeps reminding herself to put in the fridge where it will probably be forgotten, and two cans of Slim Fast—one that was supposed to be drunk for breakfast and one for lunch. She is hoping that Dave will not ask her to go eat lunch next door at the sandwich shop, but she knows she will if he asks. Her seventeen-year old son died recently in a motorcycle accident. She tells her customers—he led a good life, though.

**Claudia:** A woman who has a vague age who never has her hair styled. It is stringy and dirty-blonde. Looks as if it could use a wash, a comb-through, a color, and a style. It's strange, but she has a steady stream of customers. Dave is always offering to do her hair, but she is so busy, she can never get it done. She is married but has to work a lot of hours because her husband does not have a job. He used to work for the railroad, but he got hurt and ever since he has been trying to sue them, Burlington Northern, for disability. The disability hasn't come through yet. Her husband is taking antidepressants because he is gaining weight and because his knee hurts. He's never been hurt before. The antidepressants make him tired. She has two school-aged boys who are big.

**Vera:** The only hip person in the joint. She is always getting her hair styled—asks Dave to do it. "Whatd'ya think." Always has a date, somewhere to go and somewhere to be. She's in her early twenties. She is only working at Dave's shop because she is saving money to move to a larger city. She graduated from the hippest beauty school in the city called *Blanco & Blanco*, but they wouldn't hire her.

**Jan:** Who is still in high school and is Asian. Dave doesn't know she's only seventeen. Dave's the one who hired Jan. Jan's the manicurist who comes in. Her mother owns a salon across town, but Jan won't work there because her mother expects her to work for free. Jan only works from four to seven. Otherwise, Dave's mom takes the manicures. She is one of the few Vietnamese kids at her high school. She is way too thin, stands out on the side of the high school to smoke with her friends when she wants a smoke. She smokes Kools with menthol. Her parents don't know she's working. They think that she's involved in Speech Club at school, and they want her to learn all of the English that she can. Her father is an engineer who works for a local company, but she doesn't know really what he does for a living.

**The Other Characters**
**Rachel:** She's going through a divorce. Dave's her stylist. She has brown, silky hair, brown eyes that are big and beautiful. Kind of a Julia Roberts face, but without the big mouth. She does have a big laugh, though. Her husband met Dave playing wallyball at the local racquetball club and they've both gone to Dave for a cut or a trim ever since. She is nervous to have Dave cut her hair anymore, because she is afraid of his talking about her to her soon-to-be ex. Dave's got a crush on her, always has, and has always been up front about it in a sweet, flirtatious way. She's an aerobics instructor part-time at that local health club where they played wallyball, and she works nights at a local four-star restaurant serving cocktails.

She's been married for five years if you count this past year when she was separated, not legally. She left him on their fifth anniversary because he bought her tall plastic glasses with daisies on them to match the color of the new kitchen in their new house that she never moved into.

Ivan: Rachel's soon-to-be ex. Dave's his stylist, too, but Ivan's new girlfriend is a stylist at *Blanco & Blanco*'s, so he doesn't really ever get his hair cut by Dave anymore. He stops in to talk to Dave about Rachel on the premise that he's there to talk about cars, which is one of Dave's hobbies and one of his and Ivan's favorite topics. Ivan is tall and good-looking and has some pretty enthralling green eyes. He never runs into his soon-to-be-ex-wife there and he never thinks of her using those words to describe himself. He still thinks the words—his wife—even though he does not want to be married to her any more. He does not tell Dave that he had divorce sex with his wife in this friend of theirs, Mark's, cabin up at the local ski lodge.

Tom: Ivan's friend who lives in Ivan's new house with Ivan—the house that Rachel never lived in because she moved out before escrow closed on the house. Tom is going through a divorce, too, because his wife Morgan left him for another man. She met the guy at the local health club. The guy is the kind of guy who has muscles in his face. Tom, on the other hand, has a nice smile, nice eyes, and a fat face. He also is the kind of guy who likes a good joke—he's a businessman. He loves his kids. He has three. Two girls and a boy. His wife spoils their son. He doesn't know why. He favors his youngest child, a girl. His oldest girl is a little heavy-set, like him. They don't talk about it, though. His favorite joke ends with the punch line, "I don't have any money," and involves a woman's breasts. His wife had plastic surgery on her breasts, but it's already paid for. Tom is a customer of Tina's, but he likes to listen to Dave talk to his customers. He is also still friends with Rachel, and sometimes the two of them go to lunch together where he tells Rachel the lie that Ivan doesn't have any women over to the house. That he's really proud of Ivan. That he himself couldn't be like that.

Mark: The local celebrity in that everyone knows him, because he's the local Pepsi dealer. His dad owns the dealership. He goes to the gym: he's a body builder, he had cancer of the prostate, in his late twenties, so now he can't have sex. He can only imagine it. He can think about it. He likes Rachel—Ivan's wife, always has. He is dating other women. It's a case of poor timing. Rachel's dating some guy who looks like her soon-to-be-ex-husband. Mark doesn't get his hair cut by Dave. He only stops in to service the Pepsi machine outside of the shop and sometimes he eats at the seafood restaurant in the Alpine Village with a woman. He thinks that Rachel's messed up, but he doesn't tell her that—he just tries to be her friend. He used to drink, but now he doesn't.

Roxanne: She's young, pretty, still in college, and rooms with Rachel. Roxanne's dating Mark. Mark is a friend of Rachel's. He helped Rachel get her furniture from her husband's house. The husband was a little inebriated in the middle of the day when they went over. Mark is so big that he could lift the washing machine onto the dolly they borrowed from the Pepsi company to move Rachel's stuff. Roxanne knew Dave, Rachel's hair dresser, before Rachel because Roxanne had to take a fine arts elective at school and Dave's wife was in the show that she had to work on to fulfill her elective. Dave's wife was having an affair with the leading man, of all cliché's. Dave knew, but when Dave's wife introduced Roxanne to Dave at the final performance, she said she would go over to the shop and get her hair cut, and Roxanne is the kind of person who can listen to people's problems without passing judgement. She goes to the salon to hear Dave talk about his wife. Dave has kind of a crush on her, but she has a boyfriend whose name is Rex. People make fun of them because of their names— Rex and Roxanne. They are even the same height, so Roxanne is not sure if she wants to marry Rex. He is her college boyfriend. That is why she's dating Mark from the racquetball club, even though she knows she'll never marry him either probably mainly because of his "disability." Mark is nice to her and he takes her on plane trips down to Sante Fe and over to Seattle.

Keith: He is actually very tall. He manages the local four-star restaurant that Rachel serves cocktails at. He is thinking of letting Rachel switch to waiting tables, which could help her make about three hundred a night in tips. He waits tables, too. Ivan is one of his best friends. The waiters and waitresses play "tall wars" with Keith and Ivan after-hours by standing on the tables to see who can be taller than them. Keith gets his hair cut by Dave because his girlfriend Liv got her hair cut short there and it was very stylish. Liv goes there because Rachel told her to and Rachel's got great hair. Keith kissed Rachel one night after the bar closed down one night, a long time ago, while they were sitting down on the tile basement floor by the drain by the bathroom. He doesn't know why he kissed her, but he has been avoiding her dog tail ever since. One night he left the bar and went home and looked out the window and there was Rachel waiting in her car. He knew she wouldn't come up, though, because she didn't know which apartment was his. He lives in a senior retirement apartment on the top floor. He gets a great deal on the rent. He told Rachel she had the nicest eyes he'd ever seen.

Liv: Has great straight, reddish-brown hair, recently cut short around her ears, big glasses, and a recently developed problem with cocaine. She used to take heroin that slammed her into a wall with its effects, but she went through treatment for that. Her mother killed herself in the bathtub and her dad is a college professor at the local state university. Her father and she never talk about her mother or Liv's problems. She thinks she is not addicted to cocaine, she is only taking it to lose weight, but she does admit she really likes it. Her boyfriend Keith gets it for her, but they are only recreational users. She made a great pot of jambalaya for him one night and for Rachel, who came over while her husband was out of town. Liv knows Rachel and Keith were in the living room necking with each other while she was cleaning up. Liv refused to get dramatic, so she drank a lot of wine and went to bed, after which Keith took Rachel home and the two of them avoided having an affair together. They were all watching a movie with Jeff Bridges in it together.

Anthony: He gets his hair cut by Dave. He is an all-around nice guy who has a girlfriend in California. He is pen pals with her. Once when he was visiting Dave's shop, he passed out in the chair from a urinary tract infection. Dave tells him a little about his divorce when he says, "I wish things were different." Anthony tells him the one about shit in one hand and wishes in the other and Dave laughs. They both have nice smiles. Doesn't have a real girlfriend, never has. He works for the railroad, so moving from town to town poses a problem. His mother wants him to go back to college, but he can't commit. He met Rachel at a band concert once, a long time ago, but her husband showed up, so he moved away from her. He wanted to know her, though.

## The Other Setting
It is a racquetball club with eight courts, two of which have been converted into aerobics rooms. It has a pebbled rock floor in the entryway, a long bar that serves beer, red or white wine from a box, and bottled wine coolers. The place also sells a special kind of cookie that is fat-free and made with mocha chips. The people buy them after buying the wine and after a long workout on a Friday night and then they go out together to bars and restaurants. On Saturdays and Sundays, they participate in golf tournaments together and then they go home. There is also a Nautilus weight room upstairs with a full running track where people will reach a mile with twenty-six revolutions around the track. People stand on the track during tournaments to watch other people play down below. The place has carpeted locker rooms and a towel and lock service and is owned by a group of silent partners from a neighboring city. There is only babysitting service during the aerobics hours. Every instructor there has had or is considering having their breasts enlarged except for one named Tammy, who has naturally large breasts and Rachel, who won't on principle, but also because she doesn't have any money.

## These Characters
Nancy: Is part owner of the health club where Rachel works, doesn't like her own hair . . . ever. Has Dave barely trim it, at least every four weeks, because it grows slow. Dave tells her to leave her hair alone for a while, but she won't listen. Is considering getting a divorce because her husband took all of their savings to reinvest in his home cabinets business without her knowledge and then the business went under. Is having a quiet affair with Mark now. Even though Mark's not married, he is seeing a girl at their club. Once upon a time, had an affair with a guy named Vince from the racquet club whom she wanted to leave her husband for, but Vince never got divorced until recently. It lasted two years.

She likes Dave, but would not have an affair with him, because he is too nice and she doesn't like his glasses. Doesn't like her breasts. Is seeing a guy named Craig now, too, but nobody knows about it. She doesn't like Rachel because Rachel never gets a bad haircut and for other reasons, too.

**Nancy's best friend Susy:** Works at the racquet club, too. They are partners in doubles tournaments. She has short strong legs and very dark, kinky hair. Has been dating a black guy on and off for two years, but is sick of catching him in bed with other women. They do *not* have an understanding. Goes to the bars and out to eat with Nancy all the time. She is attracted to a guy named Craig who everyone thinks is good-looking, but he is having sex with Nancy, she knows. Craig and Nancy are sleeping in a house that Nancy bought without telling her husband. Nancy wanted a place for her mother to live, and then her mother didn't want to live there. Susy and Nancy go to the mother's new empty house one night after the bars close and they drink some more while leaning over the new Corian counter and Nancy tells her all this.

**Craig:** Plays squash instead of racquetball. Likes Rachel because she is funny and noisy and dresses sexy, but knows she is married. He is single. Nancy tried to get him in bed once, but he wasn't going. He does go places with her, though, sometimes because he has nothing better to do now that he is back home. Actually, he had an affair with Rachel a long time ago, but he doesn't tell anyone. He used to work for the post office delivering mail. Actually, with Rachel it wasn't an affair. It was sort of a one-night stand, but it was a night or two before he had to move away to London when he joined the military to learn how to be an x-ray technician to get out of that one-haircut town. He wrote to Rachel and even phoned her on Christmas Eve while he was in England, but it was getting a little too close for comfort when her husband handed the phone to her. She told him she was "trying to make a go of it." Now Craig is in love with an Asian girl he met in London, but he doesn't want to have a long-distance affair, so he came back without her. Rachel tells him that now that she is getting a divorce, she is dating someone who works in the only other nice restaurant in town, but all Craig is worried about is whether he has to watch out for her husband. Craig thinks the guy Rachel is dating looks just like her soon-to-be-ex-husband. Both guys have big noses. So does Craig.

**Dave #2:** He plays racquetball and is also an avid aerobics class attendee. He sticks his tongue out when he does the grapevine because he is concentrating. Likes to sing Elvis songs, but can't sing, even though Rachel told him once that everyone could sing. He was the second guy Rachel had an affair with, but he thinks he was the first. She tells Dave #2 that she never had an "affair" with him, because basically she left Ivan before she and Dave #2 had sex. She told herself that she would leave Ivan before she would do that again. That she would never again do that, ever. Dave #2 is a district attorney, but he won't handle Rachel's divorce case, because she won't have sex with him anymore. She says it is because she does not want to be with him, be married, or anything. She tells him she actually doesn't know what she was thinking—that she can't even read two words at a time in a book without having to put it down and cry now. Dave doesn't know what that means. Dave #2 is going bald and is seeing Rachel's therapist about his pain of getting over his relationship with Rachel.

## Another Setting

The four-star restaurant has two bars with antelope and deer prancing about in hues of mahogany, brown, and beech. The doors leading in to it are glass with brass and wood trim and there is a brass railing leading down a carpeted stairway to the basement restrooms. It is open from four in the afternoon to two—that is, the bar is open till two. The restaurant closes around ten or ten-thirty, depending on how soon the tables are turned over. The waiters and waitresses make good money there, wear polo shirts with the restaurant logo, and are all mainly either in college or have established a career in the restaurant by the time they're in their thirties. They all know each other's business and too much of it at that. They take turns seducing each other in the basement after-hours, or, if not, sniffing cocaine off the metal top of the toilet paper holder in the bathroom in the basement where they were trying to get lucky with one of the other waitresses or waiters. They speak in hip tones and subdued cool lingo; they listen to whatever's trendy, yet not too pop, and once in a while one waiter will sing out loud to the tunes piped over the bar's loudspeakers, but only if it's close to closing time and it's only regulars in the bar. The place is owned by some silent partners who live in and own another four-star restaurant in another city where Keith will go to live and work at the end of the play, and where Rachel will go visit him, nervously, to give him a final hug goodbye and ask him why they never did it, went all the way, or whatever uncool phrase she can think of at the time.

## A Few More Characters

Robyn: Works at the four-star restaurant with Rachel, Keith, and Liv. Is best friends with Liv, but really likes Rachel, too, although she knows Rachel almost had an affair with Keith while Ivan was out of town. Robyn is getting married to a guy named Dave, who is not Dave the hair stylist or Dave the lawyer. He also works at the four-star restaurant and is best friends with Ivan because Ivan services their account—Ivan's a soap salesman. It is the only four-star restaurant within a 200-mile radius, although there is another restaurant in town that ranks a three and a half. She had sex with Keith once, but her fiancé Dave doesn't know about it. Robyn told Rachel that she was selfish, selfish, selfish when she left Ivan. She told Ivan that, too. After that Robyn told her fiancé Dave that they needed to move to another town, because this place wasn't big enough. Dave is the manager and he could go work down in the Arizona restaurant that the partnership owns. Robyn has pretty caramel-colored hair and she likes to smoke pot occasionally—more than occasionally. She doesn't let Rachel stay with her and Dave when Rachel needs a place to stay, doesn't even offer. This doesn't mean she's not Rachel's friend, though.

Gene: Is part-owner of the restaurant. He is going bald. He once told Rachel not to use her finger in the foam of whipped cream to clean it up on a hot cocoa and Frangelico drink. Talks and moves nervously, checking on all aspects of the restaurant. One night, he heard Keith and Rachel in the kitchen, so he looked through the swinging door and Rachel's hair was hanging in a big swatch of bangs across her face. Gene told Keith to take Rachel home even though he had his doubts as to the sense of that. Gene has known Keith's girlfriend Liv for a long time—he never, however, sleeps with the help. He does, however, throw an elaborate party every Thanksgiving and shuts down the restaurant. He also takes everyone skiing once a year. He has met Dave the haircutter's mother once while up skiing, but he didn't care for her hair. He has also met every single one of these people in the town, because his is the only four-star restaurant within a 200-mile radius. The only other one is owned by his company of silent partners up in the northwest corner of the state in the only other major city. Doesn't know that Rachel and Keith never went all the way, that Rachel almost did, but every time she stopped herself. But judging by how she was crying in the kitchen that one night, he thinks they had an affair.

## Yet Another Setting

This is the lodge where everyone goes to ski. It has a bar for the people to drink in and a separate lodge for families and people who don't like to drink. The people in the play go to the bar setting. It is rustic. Panel-top tables, wooden chairs, a metal loop enclosure for the barmaid. Ski caps on sale behind the counter that have the logo of the ski lodge's bar on them. There is a price list of things people can buy. In there, people who've already drunk too much before going on the slopes can go and pretend to be taking a break. They order hot chocolate with Khalua in it and nachos with jalapeno peppers and sour cream on them. In the town where the lodge is located there are bars and bar nights and all the people go to these, too. They stay in the inns and in cabins there in the town. The inn buildings are shaped like A's and some people own their own cabins and they lend their keys out to their friends when they're not skiing for the weekend. There is also a famous golf course there that everyone who has money goes to golf on. This is the place that Rachel's therapist refers to as "the beginning of the end" for her, because Rachel let Dave #2 be her doubles partner in golf instead of her husband in a weekend golf tournament sponsored by the racquet club at the ski resort / golf course, and Rachel let Dave #2 kiss her in his golf cart inside someone's home garage when it started to rain and they took shelter, and then her husband threw his nine-iron on the green in front of them, just like he would throw his skis when he was mad about something, and then at the pizza place in town after the tournament, Ivan yelled at her for something, but she couldn't remember what because she had drunk nearly a pitcher of beer there. So she drove home by herself and then went over to Dave #2's, and she told him about all the other times Ivan had yelled and hit walls and gotten angry, even though that wasn't really fair, because even though those times that Ivan was yelling weren't really about anything important or weren't really related to her shenanigans at the time, because Ivan didn't really know about them then, Rachel does not tell Dave #2 about all the others. Then she and Dave #2 slept, in the literal sense, together, even though they did not have sex, yet, at that time.

## Minor Characters
A waitress
An aerobics instructor
A young woman getting her hair cut
A young woman skiing at the lodge
A young woman in a golf cart

## Act I, Scene I
The play opens five years before the play begins. Rachel is a young girl home for the summer from a year of college, where she played and drank and made the dean's list twice, despite being inebriated or hung over seventy percent of the time. Her sister has set her up on a blind date with Ivan, where they go waterskiing on a lake that everyone goes waterskiing on, and they drink beer and listen to bands like Cheap Trick and The Police and they end up holding hands on the drive home from the lake. Rachel rides with Ivan and her sister rides with her soon-to-be-ex-husband Randall.

When they get back to Ivan's hometown, which is twelve miles away from Rachel's hometown, they drink another six-pack and they wrestle on the floor, because Ivan asks Rachel where she got that scar on the back of her hand, and she shows him how she got it wrestling a guy on the floor in college. Then Ivan kisses Rachel and he takes her home and he asks her for her phone number and her address because he lives a little ways away, and Rachel is nervous and surprised as she hands her address to him on the piece of paper. She thinks it's weird that he wants her address and she doesn't think he will really write, and then he writes a letter to her in the middle of the week—a letter that is already full of love and good intentions, and it talks about her eyes and her smile and her hair and his vehicle. Then on their second date they ride on the back of a very cool, borrowed, red and black motorcycle to a pizza joint in the city where Rachel has never been, and then when someone asks Rachel at her lifeguarding job that summer, "Do you love him yet?" she has to think for a little while, but she thinks about her last date with Ivan where they went to the sand pits and floated on a big, black inner tube he had borrowed from his sister, and they were drinking beer and soaking up the sun, getting nice and brown. And then Ivan, who is tall and has skinny legs jumped out of the inner tube and his knees flashed bony in the light of the high sun as he squirted his body in angles into the smooth water. And Rachel was surprised at herself that she answered, "Yes" to her friend at the lifeguarding job. And that night when she and Ivan are kissing outside in his parents' motor home, sleeping on the pad on top of the folded down table, when Ivan tells her again, "I could fall in love with you," she answers that she could fall in love with him, too, but it was never really hesitant like that, even from the beginning. Even from the beginning, Rachel was enthralled by Ivan and she liked his green eyes and she was enthralled by the fact that he wanted to love her right away.

She doesn't know until years later in the play that they will move away to a city, far away from their two towns only twelve miles apart, and that she will be sitting in Dave's chair getting her hair cut in an A-frame building. Or that Dave will ask her, "Well, what do you want out of life, Rachel, anyway?" when she is complaining about Ivan spending money on cars again. She doesn't know that the play started long before she got to this point and that Dave is the first person who ever asked her that question, and that really it is the first time she has ever asked herself. When Dave tells her that everything is about timing and that his timing is off, she hardly listens. She lets Dave cut her hair and she looks around the beauty salon and sees all of the people cutting hair and everyone getting their hair cut when everyone's hair is really big and next year everyone's hair will be short. Dave's question goes inside her hair and she lets it rest there. It takes her many years after the play is over to get her hair cut short. Then she remembers Dave and his chair and the comfort of his scissors and his water in the bowl after coursing through her hair and the feeling of warmth it brought to her scalp and how her ex-husband always said how great it was getting your hair cut and she always wondered at his small comforts.

Rachel doesn't know at the start of play that she has Keith and Dave #2 standing around waiting to like her, too, or Mark or Craig, even Anthony, for that matter. In Act I, Scene I, Rachel thinks about Ivan's bony knees flashing in the sunlight and she tells her friend at the swimming pool that, yes, she loves him. But because she is still a good girl, she doesn't have sex with Ivan in the back of his parents' RV; she makes him wait until six months later, and then, after, she recants and says they have to wait again until after they are married another six months later. She drops out of her second year of college and they get married and they never have children, not necessarily in that order.

And she also has no idea in Act I, Scene I, that she really does love him or otherwise why would she let all the Daves in the world fuck with her head or rather that she would fuck with her own head and her own life and not really see the big picture or the play for what it was.

# Elegy

*for Ron Mitchell*

Dean Young's poem where he mentions cherry blossoms
& oblongata, then says HC's work is less lively
than a burrito,

I think the HC in question is probably Hart Crane
though with Dean Young who knows,

HC could just as easily mean TS, or JC, or PB&J,
though more likely it's a code for something else altogether.

You know, you drink some wine from a box
or play a round of mini-golf
and maybe, if you hole-in-one or hit the clown's nose,
suddenly you crack it, the code I mean, and out comes another
centipede of rhapsody and loss,

which is killing us by the way.

Not Dean Young I mean, or his poems about sorrow
and what the firmament ejaculates
on the cosmos's breasts.

Those are killing us too, but hilariously, so obviously
all is forgiven.

No, what I mean is that torn by in other words feeling
of having to bring the usual news:

about J still in love with another man no matter how much guitar
I learn, P's failed radiation treatments,
K who you never met

and what a shame because just days before he died
he was at the Christmas party making jokes
about the scary perm he wore back in the 70's.

Right away I knew that was something you would enjoy,
this good-old boy from Kentucky
who wrote songs about fishing and read everything by Larry Brown,

K standing there drinking bourbon, twirling his pistols,
a grown man speaking so freely of his hair.

And since this poem which started out as a yarn
suddenly has turned into an elegy

I might as well tell you the rest, that at the viewing I kept waiting
for K simply to spring up laughing from his box
and tell us all we could go hug his nuts.

That was hard enough.  But the really hard part was later,
smiling for his beautiful daughter, shaking his son's hand,
hugging his wife.

Afterwards I found a bar in the basement of a liquor store,
just the way K would have wanted it,
and raised my oilcans in silence while some joker at the dart board
threw one bull's-eye after another.

This next part especially I know you'll get: how I felt guilty then
of already starting this poem, trying to stanza the night
into lines I might remember more clearly later on:
the drive to Paducah, arriving first at the wrong funeral home,
the guy with the mullet outside the diner
with the all-night buffet.

Because I'd read his poems earlier that day
I wondered what Dean Young might say if he had been there,
if he had been willing to make from death something as obscene
as art,

the way I'm willing to now.

Once he was a song in his wife's lap, now he hangs over us
like a cosmic fedora, he might write
and if he'd known K at all, had loved him even a little as I did,
he'd be right.

Then another word or two about suffering, about the parade
of loss always turning into view and everyone standing there
watching, helpless with their popcorn.

Then a few more letters—Q, R, S, whoever matters most to you
put their initials here.

They stand for how hard it is to give a soul
its proper name.

# Self-Actualization

*after Mark Halliday's poem "Non-Tenured"*
*and with apologies*


It's freezing this morning
and I can sense my chapbook manuscript
descending in prestige.
Note: To hopefully publish a chapbook
called *T.S. Eliot's Codpiece*

or whatever they wore back then—
outside of retro-discos or drag shows
it certainly wouldn't be fashionable today,
breastplates or breeches or the codpiece,
though I can see each

making serious comebacks in their time,
like Jesus or Jerry Lewis,
not so much with poets or cabbies
or the stout waitress at the truck stop
near Kansas City where I stopped

to rummage the discount bin for Donna Fargo's
Greatest Hits.
No, I'm thinking of a disheveled professor,
call him Tom, who can't stop
going on about Socrates and sophists—

that guy will never read
my descending-in-prestige chapbook manuscript
that finished second three contests ago,
third two contests back,
fourth in a contest most recently that cost me

20 bucks and stamps—
but because he sat near me at the non-tenured
faculty meeting soon I was up to my codpiece
in a conversation about epideixis

and Protagoris wrapped in a charming toga
and expressing manifold ideas—
this guy Tom who probably owns horses,
who can probably recite whole sections
of *The Republic* in Greek,
who talked at me as if I were one of Rothko's

translucent, soft-edged surfaces,
eventually he said something about codification—
not the codpiece—
all of which had nothing to do
with my descending-in-prestige chapbook

manuscript.
I felt then I could safely picture his wife,
blonde, bored with endless synoptic histories
at meals and during commercials—
in my mind she was getting tennis lessons

at a resort in French Lick from some handsome
young Spaniard named Miguel—
Miguel who I imagined was like everyone else
and working on his own chapbook,
about tennis and sleeping not just with bored

housewives but also househusbands
plus the guy who comes to inseminate cows
pastured by the road—
Miguel's chapbook would be called *Kinky Messenger*
and be not only a chapbook

but also a photo journal of rhododendron.
I could hear Miguel explaining it thusly
as he messaged Tom's wife's luscious thighs
in my mind:
"darling, it's hard to know which syllables

were influenced by the yellow smoke
that rubs its muzzle on the windowpanes and which
by the grace of your backhand."
I saw my chapbook manuscript

and Miguel's in the same finalist pile at the next contest
competing with chapbooks filled with poems
that confused sexual peccadilloes
with cultivating deciduous azaleas,
poems about men's breeches in the 15ᵗʰ century
and how language pales to the experience

of men's breeches in the 15ᵗʰ century.
Tom—he was talking about Cicero then—
suddenly passed me a memo and I thought,
just slip this guy a copy
of *T.S. Eliot's Codpiece*, then he'll shut up, unerringly

atone, change the felicity
of his worldview, which is a phrase I read on the back
of another winning chapbook.
I forget the title—*Funny Face, The Happiest Girl*—
but I know things, like how the heart

can just vulcanize after too many roses
and a lover saying goodbye.
I know the boiling point for strontium—
1380 degrees Celsius—and remember what it means
to be blessed.

As soon as my chapbook manuscript
stops descending in prestige and gets published—
next week, next month, next year—
that's it, no more truck stops or toga talk,
no more faculty meetings on Wednesday afternoon.

# Memento

You should know.    Dark sunglasses.
Mutton chops    perfectly razored.  Everyone
agreed, Lily's name    should be written
in orange marmalade.    Even the stranger
on his cell phone    who stopped
long enough to nod    and smile, even the Elvis
impersonator who,    I swear it, ordered coffee,
said thank you    very much, trademark
drawl and curled    upper lip.
I think we all have    that novel squirreled
away, but in the part    of us that knows
it's hopeless to describe.    Anything.
Lightning, Randy said,    how best to describe it?
Silence.  Wisely he    raised the shade
on Lily's carryall.    I should mention
the church across    the way, the bus stop, the man
out front in Malibu    shorts talking to himself,
winning and losing    the dispute.
On the radio a piano    solo followed inexplicably
by harmonica.  Reel in    your soul,
went the lines.  Let    your name be written
in orange marmalade.    In an overstuffed
chair I read about    a woman lost in a coma,
the door popping open    and shut, open and shut,
its hinges announcing    a string of worried
costumers.  Behind the bar    black and white
photos, a guitar, Mary    running the espresso
machine, everything    whooshed and frothed.
Randy's Lily slept    soundly in her Lily carryall
on a table refinished    in yellow and red,
colors that vibrate    against one another
like a street of voices.    All of our guessing,
I thought which is    a song I still remember
the words to but    how many summers
back?    What band?

# The World

At first it wasn't appetite at all, it was a change of vision,
another one. What used to be the future, what was waiting,
what was bigger than I was, turned back and began to close in
like I was holding the wrong end of a telescope
and the world became less and less possible, less and less visible,
until my only place in it was in my body, not because I loved
or even hated it at first, but because I was alive,
because I could see nothing but my own flesh,
nothing of that first line of trees. How can I explain this?
When I picture myself then, I'm at the house on Shelter Island,
the boys gone, my parents gone,
and I'm standing at the thicket of wine berries looking out
but nothing is there. All I can feel is my flesh,
the ticking of my flesh.

# The River

You'll be gone soon and then I'll forget what I felt when the
    waterfall,
breaking the ice, changed miraculously to green in a vortex by
    the bridge,
when the ridge of pines cut their ragged blade into the sky above it.
What was that blast of light all around you?
I go back to the river, for something that will calm me
but it's always the same—
the beauty, the constant changing.

# Waking

We're apart and I've just dreamt that I was here,
the feelings real but the faces different and unknown to me.
The part I should tell you, and I wish I could tell him,
was that he finally kissed me.
We were all so tired, it was like one of those '40s dance contests,
and when we staggered into each other he held on to me and we
    kissed.
A line appeared behind my feet and we teetered over it,
falling but not hurting ourselves. Holding onto each other
we started to sleep, weirdly horizontal in a vertical plane
with people noticing and talking and walking around us.
I was torn between my shame and my intense longing.
I kept waking up and then willing myself back
to that kiss that wasn't yours.

# The Interpreter

The sky turns its back to me and to the river
while the river muscles a claw shape out of the ice
and I cross the iron bridge without jumping.
It's morning and the vapor is rising off the black water.
The black doesn't recede but advances from the field of white
and animal tracks make intricate paths around the claw
and back to the shore and back to the claw again.
If the river were a blank piece of paper,
it would have that Aboriginal quality
someone was saying was in the printmaker's work.
The sun is on the black surface in a way I can't describe
but it feels like the brilliance goes right to my heart
like the arrow did when we played Cowboys and Indians
by clutching our chests and keeling over.
I turn the corner onto an embankment of snow
and it's dotted with prisms,
each flashing an incredible signal
I don't know how to receive.

# Stockbridge

That was another winter.
Was anyone with me? I don't remember.
In the car, I recognized the road there
like you recognize music without remembering the lyrics.
It was February.
Maybe that's why it comes to me now.
The blue everywhere, the first blue, the last.
The pines with their black towers.
The branches of maples with their infuriating nakedness.
How is the struggle coming?
I live with you and want others.

# Floating

Jed says summer starts on Memorial Day, and I believe him because at school we never do anything but watch videos and erase marks from our books after that. So it's really the first day of the summer when I see Shane Spangler lounging next to the lifeguard stand waiting for his shift on the chair to begin. I've been coming to Elk Run Pool with my stepsister three summers in a row. The first summer we could only go in the shallow end and the game room, but now Darla's 13, and Jed says that's old enough she ought to be able to keep us out of trouble. We live on the far side of the trailer park, where there's another hill in back with an old turkey house. Now it's full of moldy hay bales, and one time we found the skin of a black snake.

I saw Shane all those other summers. He used to stand me and Darla up on his shoulders, and his fingers would feel slippery around our ankles, and he'd jump off into the deep end and send us flying. He'd come up first and pull himself out of the pool and stretch out his hand like to help me up. Then he'd fling me back into the water and say, "Come on now, Casey. You got to hang on," until I got mad and had to doggy paddle it over to the ladder, with him doing his damn donkey laugh. Back then he and his friends were all buzz cut and shiver ribs and drippy cut-off jeans.

So it's Memorial Day weekend. That's when they always open up the pool in Shelby. We already wasted half the day in town because Mama wanted to watch the parade. Then Jed saw his buddies from Walker, and we all had to go into the Vista Grill and suck on French toast sticks while he had a few beers. Darla and I are in such a hurry we make it up the steps before Jed turns off the car.

"Hey, shut that thing right," Jed yells when we leave the screen door swinging. But I saw him in the car, rubbing his big fingers in the back of Mama's hair the way he does when he's had just enough of his beers, and I know he's not mad for real.

I got two new suits from the attic shop. That's what Mama calls it when I wear Darla's old clothes. My stepsister's just finishing up the eighth grade, and she's started growing boobs, so nothing fits her anymore. One's a red and white two-piece with a big rose in the center of the top, and that's the one I put on. I'm feeling pretty good as I set to untangling our bikes from the mess of junk under the deck until Darla comes out in her new lavender bikini with the ties on the side, looking all slick and slinky and curved. I figure I'll still beat her to the pool, so I hop on my bike and take off pedaling, even on the down hills. There was a thunderstorm last night. Now the sun's breaking through, and the water's starting to sizzle in the potholes. The rain wilted the lilacs in the pool lady's yard, and they smell sticky and heavy like to make you sick.

As soon as I lean my bike against the chain link fence, I realize Darla has all our money, so I'll have to walk in with her anyway. I can see her coasting down the hill with her ponytail flying straight and blond behind her, and that makes me madder because I cried till Mama let me cut off my hair last year, and now it's all poofy curly around my head. It's in knots most of the time because it hurts too bad when Mama tries to comb it. Jed calls it my red rat's nest, but Mama says my hair's not red, it's auburn. Which everyone knows is much less trashy. I sit down and stare at the kiddie pool through the metal fence and start picking through the clover thinking maybe I'll find a four-leafer, and that's when I see him.

He's at the base of the stand wearing those red shorts they make all the lifeguards wear at Elk Run Pool. His hair's grown out, and there are damp curls of it hanging down the back of his neck. He's got sunglasses dangling around his chest on a rubber string next to a whistle chain. I'm not sure it's Shane Spangler until he donkey laughs at something the blond haired girl says up in the chair.

"What're you staring at?" Darla wants to know when she pedals up not even out of breath.

We walk over to the counter, and she pulls a wad of ones out of the front pocket of her cut-offs. She's got them held together with a lavender and pink glitter hair barrette, and I think that looks pretty posh, but I sure don't tell her. Odessa, the pool lady, puts down her cigarette to count our money. Two times she counts out those dollar bills. She's real tan and skinny, but her arm is all shaky-sag underneath when she finally waves us inside.

Her husband's a lot older. He worked in the muffler factory with Jed, but he got hurt in some kind of accident and doesn't ever come outside. They got a load of money—that's what Jed said—because of that accident, enough to buy the pool when the town couldn't afford to keep it open any more. They got the whole pool and the campground next to it and the trailer park up the hill where we live. Their house isn't any bigger than our trailer, though. It's a little brick thing, painted white, right as you start up the hill. They always got all the blinds closed. Odessa walks up and down the hill pumping her arms and shaking her butt every evening. She holds a little dumbbell in one hand and a cigarette in the other, and every time she gets back to the bottom of the hill she switches them.

"Hey Hinkles!" yells Odessa behind us as our flip flops slap across the cement. "You two better stay out of trouble this summer." She's got stringy brown hair, and she looks like a muppet when she starts screaming. We don't look back because we know most of the stuff she's always accusing us of isn't even our fault. Last summer we tried to tell Jed that she was a grumpus and he needed to come down here and stop her from picking on us. Mama laughed and said it's because she's getting old and she's not getting any from her old man since his accident. They wouldn't tell me any what, and Darla rolled her eyes and told me to shut up.

"Well lookie here. It's Darla Hinkle and Miss Casey," says Shane when we walk under his chair. My sister doesn't look up, but I flip him the bird as we pass. Shane Spangler just shakes his head and laughs. Last summer that would've been enough to set him after me to throw me in the deep end, but I figure he's got his duties now.

Darla wants to spread our towels out on the grassy end where there's a mess of picnic tables and grills. I can see there's already a bunch of high school kids sitting over there smoking and playing their radio. I say no way—I got stung by a bee next to that trash can last summer. When she gives me that prissy eye roll, I tell her go on over there by herself, but she says Jed told her to stay with me. So we put our towels on the smooth cement by the deep end, and she's got to get every wrinkle out of her towel before she'll lie down on the thing. She's that way, Darla is. Right off she starts oiling herself up. And by the time she settles down, you'd think she was trying to climb into a too hot bathtub, it's such a show. I try to be still for a while because I know she'll want to sunbathe before swimming, and I can tell she's kind of mad at me flipping off Shane and not wanting to put my towel on the grass.

My sister can lie in the sun for hours and not get burnt, even though she's got blond hair. Mama and her friend Janelle say that's unusual to get so tan, with the blond hair and all. My skin turns bright pink, and Mama rubs me down with Noxema and pieces of aloe plant from the pots along the deck. The first summer we came to the pool by ourselves was the worst because I wouldn't let Darla put lotion on me. We swam for nine hours that Memorial Day, and that night it felt like my skin was shrinking around me. Mama smacked at my hands when I tried to reach them around to rake my back. She made me wear a T-shirt to the pool. I yanked that thing off once we got here, and when we were lying on our bellies in the grass, Darla pulled the pieces of dead skin off my shoulders for me. They were like little snake skins. We crinkled our noses as she tossed them up into the air and watched them float down like insects.

Pretty soon I can't help but start in. "Come on," I say "This is boring as shit. Let's go off the slide." There's a huge metal slide at the Elk Run Pool.

"Don't cuss," says Darla without moving or opening her eyes.

This coming from the girl who got a week of in-school suspension up at the middle school for telling the student teacher for gym class to put a field hockey stick up her ass. I know why she won't go down the slide. Before the parade, she spent about an hour curling her bangs into a crunchy pouf that's shining like a Brillo pad on the top of her head. I can't help it then. I start making my I-want-my-own-way noises. I make them with my nose, and they're better than crying on Mama and Jed. But Darla just rolls her head toward me and says, "Jesus, Casey, stop whining. I'm not getting in yet. Go down yourself."

I can see the thing looming across the deep end, about as big as a roller coaster. It doesn't just drop you off into the pool. It spits you out about ten feet, with your butt skidding like a big rock on top of the water.

"You're supposed to stay with me."

"I can see you," she says with her eyes still shut.

When I get over there, there's a woman already standing on the wooden platform up at the top, pulling at the back of her

117

bathing suit and hollering at a guy who's sitting on the side of the pool. She finally shuts her mouth and grabs hold of the bar, and for a minute I just hear the splashing of the little jet of water before she goes screaming down the chute. She disappears beneath the surface, and a few seconds later I see her hanging onto the side of the pool. I can tell she got a nose full of water even though she's trying to act like everything's okay.

I figure I'll wait a little while, so I make my way down to the shallow end where you can go in easy. It's so cold I'm all chicken-skinned before the water's up to my waist. I can see the hairs prickling on my legs beneath the water. I'm going to tell Mama I need a razor like Darla. I stand there cross-armed for a minute trying to figure out who I want to play with. There are a lot kids from school around, but I don't see anybody from my class. Two boys are throwing a Wiffle ball back and forth across the water, and when they overthrow it lands near me. I scoop it up as the water starts seeping into the holes to sink it. I'm about to say what's your name to the nearest boy when the other one yells, "Hey you girl! Give that back. Hey lifeguard," he says, "She stole our ball."

Shane turns around to look at us, and right as he goes to blow his whistle I chuck that ball over the fence.

He makes me come over to the stand, and when I get there he calls me Miss Meanness and wants to know why I threw their ball.

So I say, "Cause my sister won't go down the slide with me."

He looks down the sidewalk to where Darla's lying, all greased up with one knee propped in the air.

"Well go on and get it and give it back to them. Then when I get my break in about ten minutes I'll go down the slide with you."

I do like he says, but when I get around to the back side of the fence I can see they haven't cut the grass yet this year, and I'm not wearing my flip flops. There's a mess of dandelions and Queen Anne's Lace, all of it swarming with bees, so I've got to pick my way through all careful before I can even find the thing. I finally see it, and I grab it and hold it up in the air for Shane to see. When he nods his head, I toss it back over the fence, but I make sure those boys will have to swim for it.

Shane has climbed down from his chair, and that blond-haired girl's climbing back up. He hangs his whistle chain and his sunglasses off the ladder, and he says let's go.

Over at the ladder he does this little bow thing and says, "After m'lady." I just stand there looking up. Nobody's at the top this time, and I can hear the little jet of water whistling out. I start to feel like all those bumble bees on the other side of that fence are buzzing around inside my stomach, but I don't want Shane to think I'm chicken shit, so I step up to the ladder. Big shade trees on the other side of the fence keep the metal from getting too hot, and the steps have grippy teeth, and I know Shane's coming up right behind me.

I'm not really scared of the slide anyway, so much as cautious. Jed taught me how to go down it last summer after watching five or six times as I had to shimmy back down the ladder to where Shane Spangler and his crowd of boys were booing and laughing. He told me we weren't going home until I went down that slide. He said there's a secret to liking heights, and that's to not ever look down, only up or out. He said that before he met my mama, when he and Darla were living on the farm taking care of Doug Eppard's cows, she would climb all the way up the silo, and she was way littler than me. Jed says he doesn't want his girls to be scared of anything, and I know that must be true because Darla's not scared of much. Of course you wouldn't think it now, not the way she acts so prissy.

So I don't look down, even once I'm up on the platform. I look up at the swirly kind of clouds, the kind that Jed says make for good sunsets, and I look out across the pool for my stepsister. I figure I'll wave at her and make nice, but she's not on her towel. She probably went to the bathroom to check on her bangs. I don't swing myself off the bar or anything. I'm not scared, but I'm not taking any chances. I just scoot my bottom along the metal until I start moving. I don't grip at the sides because even though Darla has told me a zillion times I'm not moving fast enough, it feels like it could cut my hand for sure. I use both hands to hold my nose shut. For a second I hang there with the treetops floating in front of me over in the campground. Then my belly drops out and the clouds rise up, and I close my eyes as tight as I can. By the time I'm bobbing in the water I can see Shane never climbed up the ladder at all. He's leaning against it talking to my sister.

"Shane Spangler," I holler, "You're a goddamn liar."

"I was watching you," he says. "Besides, now you know you can go down all by yourself, and you don't have to be scared no more."

"I wasn't scared!"

Darla's rolling her eyes, and he's telling me I got to exit on the left side so I don't get in the way of the divers. I can't give him the finger because if anything messes up my doggy paddle I get a monster nose full of water, so I paddle right across the row of diving boards to the opposite side of the pool like I never even heard him. He looks at Darla like to ask why I'm so bad, and she just shrugs her shoulders. Then they go off to the game room to play pool.

My stepsister doesn't know how to play pool. Besides, who plays pool when they could be swimming? Last summer me and Darla and Shane and his friends would only go to the game room to play Pole Position II or else the pinball machines, and then only if it was raining. I think I'm not going talk to her again or at least not until tonight, but I mess up when we get out to the parking lot and she wants to know where we left our bikes. When we're walking them up the hill, she asks me why I was so peeved back there. I don't know how to tell her she's fixing to ruin the whole summer.

Mama has Wednesdays off. The dentist office where she's an assistant closes down all day. Jed says it's the cheapest way Dr. Leubner knows to get girls to work for him on Saturdays. So it's Wednesday, and me and Darla and Mama are having our hair done at J. & Company on Main Street. "J" stands for Janelle. She's a friend of Mama's who always lets all three of us get our hair done together. She has purple eye shadow and shaggy black hair. She smells spicy when she leans over the sink to lather up your head, and she grows her nails out way long so they give your scalp a good scratching. She's pretty posh with long silver earrings and jingle bracelets and stuff. She sits Mama and Darla down with a magazine and tells them that after she finishes with me there's something she's got to talk to them about.

I always have to go first, otherwise Janelle says I can't sit still long enough for her to finish giving me a trim. She tried to talk Mama out of cutting my hair off last winter, but Mama told her go

ahead and hack it because she was tired of arguing with me. Janelle
has to make my hair straight to cut it even. She puts a bunch of
goop on it after she's done washing and takes the blow dryer to
little chunks of it until it lays all soft and fluffy around my chin.
Once she starts snipping I can see the clumps of hair gathering on
the linoleum out of the corner of my eye, and they look all straight
and pretty. I start to whimper because I know they are way too
long, and I won't ever be able to get my hair back in a ponytail
now, so finally I yell, "Stop."

"My God that girl's got lungs," Janelle says to Mama. Then
she spins the chair around so they can both look at me.

"You need to use the ladies room?" I can tell Mama is hoping
that's all this is going to be.

"No!" I smooth my hair down next to my head and hold my
hands there so Janelle can't get to it.

"Well what's the problem then?" Mama is standing up now.

"I changed my mind. I don't want it cut."

"Well it's a little late. I already finished this entire side."
Janelle points to the shortened half of my hair with her little silver
scissors. "Do you want to go around with your hair hanging two
different lengths?"

"She probably wouldn't mind." That's Darla, sticking her
nose into my haircut.

"Casey, I thought you wanted long hair again." Mama's
talking slow, the way she does when she's about to start yelling.
"Look, if you don't trim it then it won't grow. It's up to you."

Janelle scoops some of the reddish brown fluff off the floor
and waves it in front of my face. "Sweetie, that's all I'm taking off.
That'll grow back in a month."

I let go of my head and take the trimmings from her. When
no one's looking I slide them under the black cape she has covering
me and into the pocket of my shorts.

Later I try looking at magazines, but they never have
*Highlights* or *Ranger Rick* like at the doctor's office, only the kind
of magazines that Darla's been buying at Rite Aid and taking to
the pool all summer. Janelle can't believe how tall Darla's grown
when she sits down in the chair or that all the sparkly streaks in
her hair just come from the sun.

"You wouldn't believe how many girls come in here wanting
me to highlight their hair to look like that," she says. "And I can't

do it. You're a lucky one." I know Darla squeezes lemon juice on her hair every morning before we go to the pool. I think about asking Janelle has she tried that.

"In fact," says Janelle, looking at Mama, "I've been thinking she should enter the Miss Field Day Pageant."

Shelby Field Day comes every August. There's a big parade. The Lion's Club men and the cheerleaders from up at the high school where Darla's going to be in the fall and a bunch of the churches decorate hay wagons and pick-up trucks and throw candy. I got a load last year—of course it's mostly that pick-a-mix stuff from the plastic bins at Food Lion. There's a big fair too every year, with funnel cakes and a scrambler ride down in the park. There's even a Ferris wheel that Jed always goes on with me. He takes us on Wednesday because kids can ride all night if they pay five dollars for a little red bracelet.

"Have you ever thought about doing the pageant?" Now Janelle's asking my sister.

"I don't know. Some of the girls from school are doing it."

"Isn't it kind of pricey?" Mama asks. "With a big entry fee and then a dress. I can't really see Jed going for that."

"Well, we could sponsor you," Janelle says. "All those girls have sponsors. We do someone every summer. We do her hair and make-up and pay the entry fee. Then when they call her out they say our name too, and we get a little advertising." She leans down to look over Darla's shoulder into the mirror. "You could be the J. & Company girl."

When I hear that I go rearrange all the bottles in the nail polish display.


For Shane's sixteenth birthday he gets a new truck—a Chevy S10 with a little seat in the back—and on his break he asks us do we want to go for a ride. When he goes to get his keys out of his locker, I tell Darla there's no way I'm going with him because Jed says we're supposed to ride our bikes to the pool and straight back with no lollygagging.

"Well I'm the boss of you when we're here," she says.

The back seat of his truck is so small you have to sit sideways. He says to buckle up, but before I can my head starts bumping against the window because he tears across the potholes, leaving dust and gravel floating above the Elk Run Pool parking lot. I watch Route 33 snake out behind us through the back window, and every now and then I hear Darla laugh about something going on up front. We're heading back towards Shelby, which I can't figure out since Bear Gun and Grocery is just half a mile up from the pool, and that's where Jed and Mama always go. Sometimes they just walk up there for no reason in the evening and bring us back candy bars. Shane turns into the 7-Eleven in town and gets out. He pulls the seat up and hands me a five-dollar bill.

"You want to go get us some cokes?" He stands there with his hand on the back of the seat, and I have to squeeze past him to get out of the truck. I can see the little circle of hair beneath his arm.

"Casey, get me a diet." Darla's started thinking she's got fat thighs.

Inside the store there's a girl standing at the ice cream counter. She's jiggling a baby on her hip and talking to the woman behind the counter about someone they both know and trying to figure out whether she wants strawberry or pistachio. That baby's slurping at his fingers, and every now and then she leans over and shhhhhh's in his ear. I have to make my way through the candy aisle to get to where the sodas are.

Mama doesn't trust me to go into the store all by myself, especially because of all the townies that like to hang out, so I hesitate at the front for a second, feeling my palm start to sweat around that five dollar bill. I look back through the door for Shane's red truck, but there's really nothing to see since he's got those dark windows. I can hear the women blabbing it up over at the ice cream counter, so I grab a handful of fire balls as I pass by and stuff them real quick inside my back pocket. When I get to the cooler the doors start fogging up as soon as I open them, and I don't want that lady to come over and get after me for messing up the glass, so I just grab three bottles and head over to the counter. I know I ain't in any trouble for that candy because the woman behind the counter keeps on talking and baby cooing even as she's ringing me up.

"Casey, this ain't diet." My sister does that prissy eye roll as Shane hands her a bottle and I climb back into the little sideways seat.

"Well, Darla, you ain't fat." I can't see what he does, but my sister starts laughing and squirming toward the window.

My sister hears the crinkling of the wrapper as I pull out one of those fire balls. She wants to know where did I get that candy and did I use Shane's money.

He starts to say that's okay, but I thrust what's left between their two seats.

"There!" I say, "Count your stinking change. I used my own money."

"You don't have any money. Jed gave it to me this morning." I can tell by my sister's voice that she knows about the candy. She can't tell on me though because we weren't supposed to be leaving the swimming pool.

When we pull back onto the highway, I see that the candy's not really important anyway, that for some other reason things are different than before I got out of the truck. The two of them are quiet all the sudden, and Shane's got his arm stretched out so that his hand is lying on the headrest of Darla's seat. I use my thumb to pull back my middle finger, and I give him a good thunk right on the knuckle. He swings his head around and smirks at me, but he doesn't move his arm.

"Hey," I say, "Ain't you supposed to have both hands on the wheel?"

When I get home I climb up the hill to the old turkey house before it starts getting dark. Inside it smells like year-old hay and sawdust, but there's a far away smell too, of animals and weather. Last summer me and Darla—and sometimes Shane and the boys from the pool—would play in here all the time, hay tunnels and capture-the-flag and stuff, even though Mama was always afraid we might get hurt and wanted us to act more like ladies. I tried to get Darla to come up here the first rainy day this summer, but she says it's not fun anymore. I can kind of see what she means because most times when I come up here now I just sit and spy down the hill through the air vents. You can see all the way to Odessa's, where the dark windows in the front reflect the sunlight like mean-looking eyes. Last summer we spent a lot of time hiding out here from the pool lady, although she never was really looking for us. We figured her husband's worse than her, even, lying on the bed with twisted up legs.

I shimmy myself up onto the rounded side of one of the hay

bales by pulling at the twine that's holding it together. It's old and moldy and sometimes it tears apart in your hands. I crawl across the hay until I find the pile of feathers I use to mark my spot. They're pigeon feathers not turkey—that's all that lives in here now. I showed some of them to Jed, and he's the one that told me. I reach down between two bales, carefully, because, like I said, one time we found a snake skin, and pull out one of Jed's old hunting socks. I dump the rest of those fire balls inside with my important stuff. I wiggle my fingers around inside, making sure everything's still there. I got some of my hair, a rock from last time we went fishing over at Lake Moomaw, some change I saved from my tooth pillow and chores and stuff, and an arrowhead that Jed gave me.


That night we cook hamburgers out on the grill, and as we're sitting at the picnic table eating them, Darla starts talking about some movie. "It's about this guy who's doing a science project," she says, "and he discovers how to make himself invisible."

I know what movie she's talking about. In the commercials the invisible guy gets to follow this girl around, even to the bathroom and slumber parties and stuff. I glare at her across the table.

"Anyway, there's this guy at the pool who wants to go see it, too." She's just nibbling at a veggie burger because she's thinking maybe she doesn't want to eat meat anymore. I can tell by the way she's chewing that thing must taste awful bad.

"Since when do thirteen-year-old girls go on dates?" asks Jed.

"What exactly is she asking?" Mama wants to know.

"I want to go into Garrison and go see a movie with Shane Spangler." We don't have a movie theater in Shelby, so we have to drive half an hour to Garrison if we want to see a show. Sometimes I get to feeling car sick on the way back, especially if I eat too much candy.

Mama's looking at Jed with her eyebrows raised up all funny. "Would the Spanglers drive you two love birds, or would we have to?"

"He's going to drive us. He just got his license and a new truck."

"All that means is that he's too old for you." Jed says through a mouthful of hamburger. "You can't go on that kind of date."

They all three get to talking at once, and Darla's voice starts cracking. So I pick through the pile of grilled burgers, slicing them all open a little the way Mamma never lets me, until I find one with just the right amount of pink in the middle.

Later, after they've sent me to bed I'm standing in the hallway brushing my teeth, trying to catch a glimpse of the TV, and I can hear Darla talking real low to someone on the phone in her room, sniffling a bit every now and then. I stand there until Mama hollers for me to go on and get in bed. Then I yell back there's no way I can go to sleep because Darla's still blubbering on the phone. They have a rule about how she's not allowed to talk on the phone after ten o'clock. When I hear her getting up, I run for my room and close my eyes like I'm sleeping.

I'm floating in the shallow end with my arms spread wide, head down, hair fanned out all around my eyes. In the water my hair looks longer and straighter. It's Wednesday, and Mama took Darla to Garrison to look for a Miss Field Day dress. That means I've got nobody here watching me, so I'm supposed to stay out of the deep end.

Jed taught me to float like this when he gave me swimming lessons. He would lay his hand flat underneath my belly and balance me right at the top of the water and say for me to relax. When I finally did he'd pull his hand away real slow, so I wouldn't even know it was gone, and sure enough I'd hang right there at the surface like a fishing bobber. He says anybody can float if they try, that the only reason for people drowning in pools and lakes is because they get scared. I haven't tested the floating thing enough to try it in the deep end, though. There I always try to hit the water doggy paddling.

I saw them fish a boy out of the water at the boat landing at Lake Moomaw. Jed's boss took us fishing, and we were coming in for the day. There was a bunch of commotion so we hung back a ways from shore with the boat engine making colors swirl on top of the water. The boy was bigger than me. Later, Jed told Mama he was about Darla's age. He was floating just like Jed showed me, but he never turned his face up out of the water. Two men pulled him in and stretched him out over the grass. As soon as Jed and his boss walked the boat up onto the trailer, Jed pulled me out by my arm pits and stood me on the gravel.

"Casey, go get in the car right now." He handed me the keys, and when I turned and stared at the men kneeling over top of the boy, he shoved my backside. "Girl, I said go get in the car."

LeAnn Wharton comes over and tries to float with me, but she can't do it right because she keeps talking. She's splashing around between me and the lifeguard stand.

Do I want to go under water and have a tea party she wants to know. I don't say anything because I'm playing like that drowned boy. "Do you want to dive for pennies?" I can hear her voice even with my ears under the water. It makes me think of at school this past year how she would try to make all of us fifth grade girls do cheers with her out on the playground. I could hear them chanting even on the days I was in trouble and sitting cross-legged facing the brick wall. "How about if I let you use my new diving mask and I use my sister's goggles? Then do you want to?"

LeAnn's got cheerleader twin sisters up at the high school. Darla's been talking to them a lot at the pool this summer because she's thinking maybe she's going to try out for cheerleader in the fall. They both have boyfriends, and they float around the edge of the deep end holding onto them like they can't swim or something. I've seen them with their mouths locked, and I think it must probably taste like chlorine to kiss on a boy in the pool like that. One time I asked my sister had she kissed Shane.

"What do you think?" she smirked.

"I bet you do, and I bet Jed would get mad. It looks so dumb anyway. Why'd anybody want to just sit there with their face hooked onto some boy's?"

"You don't just sit there," she rolled her eyes. "You touch your tongues and stuff."

"Nasty!" I made gagging noises to show her how disgusting that was.

"If you ever grow up you won't think so."

I don't want to try it for real, but sometimes when I'm in my room or else up the hill at the turkey house I try kissing on my hand. Or if nobody can see my face, like when I'm floating in the pool this way, I try turning my tongue over on itself inside my mouth. Just to see how it would feel to touch it against another tongue.

All of a sudden I feel someone yanking at the straps of my swimsuit.

"Hey!" I jerk up with my arms flying. I slick my drippy hair back out of my face. I know it's Shane with his red shorts and whistle chain. He drags me over to the side of the pool by my straps and sits me up on the warm cement. He's fired up and wagging his finger in front of my face. What's wrong with me he wants to know, and haven't I ever heard of the boy who cried wolf? When he tells me I have to sit out of the pool for twenty minutes, I figure I'll just get my bike and ride home.

Back at the trailer I have to squeeze into the bathroom sideways because Darla's standing naked in a puddle of pink satin. Her arms are folded across her chest like she doesn't want me to see her, but it's just smooshing her boobs up making them look even bigger. She twists herself around trying to see her bottom in the mirror. "That one makes me look too wide in the rear."

"Well I think it might be too big, and I don't know about the sequins on this one." Mama's perched on the edge of the toilet, and she fingers the dress that's lying across her lap. "Casey, you want to help us make a decision?"

I roll my bathing suit down to my calves then kick my feet free. I sit down on the tub to look at my toenails. They're turning kind of yellow. I thought I might have some kind of toe disease, but Mama says it's just from the chlorine and running around without shoes all the time.

Darla pulls another gown from the counter and hoists it over her shoulders.

"Did you see Shane at the pool?" Her voice is muffled by all the material.

"No."

"Really? He's supposed to be working today."

Mama says I've got a lying problem, and that may be so because sometimes I'm not sure why I say things the way I do. I better start fixing it though because the Presbyterian Church has vacation Bible school this month, and they let you play dodge ball and make sculptures with matches.

I ask Mama how'd she afford so many dresses. We're not poor. One of the Sluss girls was in my class last year. There's a Sluss in almost every grade, and some grades have more than one because a couple of the boys have failed. She didn't have but two changes of clothes. That's poor. We're saving, and that's different than poor. We've been saving money to build a house ever since Mama got married to Jed. They keep all the bills in a green shoebox underneath the counter, and every so often they dump everything inside out onto the kitchen table. I know they won't be going on one of their walks on those evenings.

"I charged them, nosey," says Mama. "But we have to take two of them back this evening. We couldn't decide, so we figured we'd ask you and Janelle." She plucks my rolled up bathing suit off the floor like it's poison and tosses it in the tub. "That means we definitely don't want them to get wet."

Darla's worked the last gown over her head and she's trying to get it fastened. This one's a shade lighter than the others, and it shimmers when she moves, like insect wings.

I stand up on the edge of the tub where I can see into the mirror on the medicine cabinet. I put my hands on my hips and suck in my stomach until my middle looks lean and stretched out like Darla's. I turn sideways and look at myself until I have to breathe. Then my belly bows out like a bubble.

"So which one do you think?" my sister asks. I say I don't really like any of them, but when I look up at her she's turning in a circle in front of the mirror holding her arms out wide, and I see she looks like Cinderella.

For the next two weeks that dress is hanging in the coat closet. Mama's got it wrapped in layers of plastic. Whenever I walk by, I remember it's in there hanging like the squirmy webs of tent worms in the trees around the turkey house. I think about sneaking in there during the day while Darla's yapping on the phone or sitting on the toilet and maybe plucking off one of the pearl buttons. I could hide it up the hill in my sock and nobody'd ever know, but I can't get past opening the door. That shimmer material is all wound around itself and then covered in plastic like the pink underside of a shell. It makes me feel crowded.

A lot of stuff's been making me feel that way lately. The cloud of Love's Baby Soft perfume my sister's always leaving in the bathroom. The tissues with pink lipstick marks piling up in the wastebasket and stuffed into the ashtray in the car.


Darla keeps her foam hair curlers under the bathroom counter. She's got them stashed in a suitcase her real Mama forgot when she left her and Jed. It's one of those old-fashioned round ones with hinges that snap it shut and a brass clasp that's pretty posh. I figure I'll load it up instead of my knapsack because it's way more stylish, plus sturdier, and I'm not sure how long I'll be on the road.

I make my exit when Darla's tanning out on the back deck. She's got the ribbons to her bikini undone because she's got a strapless dress, and Janelle says the judges count off for tan lines. I bring my special sock down from the turkey house. I load it along with an apple and six granola bars into that little suitcase.

Under the coffee table we've got a mess of maps. I pull one out that says *George Washington National Forest, Deerfield Ranger District* across the side. When I unfold it I can't make any kind of sense of it, and I'm sorry I tried because it's a chore to fold that thing back up, but I throw it into my suitcase with the other stuff. I leave all those pink rollers piled on the linoleum floor. I'm a little disappointed that they didn't clatter more or roll behind the toilet when I dumped them out.

I can't take my bike because I'm only allowed to ride it around the trailer park and up and down our road. I can cross the highway, but only to get to the pool. I'm pooped by the time I make it half way down the hill. Darla and I already rode our bikes down once today and then walked them back up. I sit down on one of the white-washed rocks marking the end of Odessa's driveway.

I'm feeling brave because I know the pool lady's still down there behind the counter, making change and scooping snow cones. I unwrap one of my granola bars, and I'll be damned if it isn't a peanut-butter one. I ate too much peanut butter the year before last when I was in the fourth grade. I had one every day that Mama packed my lunch, and I'm tired of peanut butter. Well, I try it anyway because Jed says every so often it's a good idea to try some food you don't like, just in case your tastes have changed without your even knowing it. Mine haven't, so I spend a while trying to spit that taste out of my mouth, and once I see the way my spit looks when it splatters against the black driveway, I keep doing it.

"If you use the hose, that job'll probably go faster." Those words come out of nowhere, and for a second I think about God talking to Abraham and God talking to Moses and God talking to all those other people at the vacation Bible school. I see somebody standing inside the dark rectangle of the front doorway, and I suck in my breath real hard because I know it's got to be the pool lady's husband, and that's worse than God. He asks me do I want to come inside and have a coke.

Now, I don't get cokes too often on account of Jed says they make me hyperactive. Even with all that spitting I still have a mouthful of peanut butter, and there's nothing like a coke to get rid of a nasty taste in your mouth. So I walk right up the steps and the pool lady's husband points me inside with his cane. It's not really a cane but more like a walking stick, carved up to look like a snake. It's just the kind of thing I figured he would have except it's got some kind of jewel where the eyes are, which is pretty posh for an invalid man. I sneak a look around as I'm following him through the living room. They don't have a sofa, just two big black leather recliners in front of a TV that's so big I don't even see it at first.

He's got to shift his stick to the other hand when he opens the refrigerator. He pops the top of my coke after he sets it on the table, and he pulls out a Coors Light for himself. "This is my silver coke," he says. Then he holds out his hand and says his name is Whitey.

I don't know if that means Mr. Whitey or Whitey and then Mr. something else, so I just shake his hand and say, "Casey Hinkle." Then he looks me over and asks me where it is I'm heading today.

"I'm heading over to the lake," I say. Then I tell him probably Lake Anna or Lake Moomaw when he wants to know which one.

"What are you going to do there?"

I'm thinking he's awfully nosey for an invalid, but he gave me a coke, so I don't want to be rude. "I'm going to take a job as a professional fisherman," I say.

"Oh, well, I do a lot of hunting and fishing myself," he says.

I tell him straight out then that I don't believe him because everyone knows he never leaves his house.

He thinks that's pretty funny. "Sometimes I do," he says when he's done laughing. "Only I don't tell anyone where I'm going."

"Not even the pool lady?"

"The pool lady?" he laughs. "Well, sometimes I might tell her." He's got a gray beard that's longer than I'm used to seeing and hair that's combed back with grease so that it's a little bit darker. His eyes are pale blue. "I got to keep some secrets," he says.

He asks me do I want to see another secret, and I say I guess I do. I have to follow him down the hall with his cane making a thump-scrape-thump that's still kind of scary. He opens a door at the end of the hallway, and inside there's a lighted table and workbench. Along one wall there are shelves with clear sliding trays, and I can see they're full of feathers, wire, glass beads, and tiny bottles of paint.

I ask him is this his craft room.

"You could say that," he says. "This is where I make my lures."

"Lures?"

"Sure, fishing lures," he says. "I make them myself. I'll show you." He limps over to the table and dangles one from his fingers beneath the lamp. It's larger than I would have thought. I'm used to the rubber and plastic lures Jed buys at Wal-Mart. They're all shaped liked crayfish, worms, or little frogs. This one's more like a piece of jewelry. It has a silver shield at the top like Jed's spinners, but it rests on a mess of feathers and beads that glow all kinds of pastels when he shakes it in the light.

"I can't see nobody catching anything with that," I say.

"Oh, I catch some big ones."

"Well then let's see them." Jed's got two big fish he caught mounted on the living room wall back at the trailer and probably ten more sliced up in plastic bags in the freezer.

"I never keep them," he says. "They look so much prettier swimming around, and the pool lady," he looks at me and winks when he says that, "is not much good at cooking fish."

I tell him I better get going seeing as how I still got a long way to go yet today.

"Why don't you go on home," he says. "I tell you what, you keep that lure because I always have good luck with that kind. But don't go off to be a professional just yet. Come back down here and visit me again, and you can help me make some more. Then you'll be ready for the tournaments."

I shake the lure in front of me in the fading light as I trot back up the hill. I decide it's the kind of treasure I should keep with me instead of in my sock. I watch it shimmer, and I like the way it feels to have a secret.

It's a Sunday night, and Jed's holding our seats in the auditorium. I'm disappointed because I figured that if this pageant is part of Field Days there would at least be cotton candy. Mama forced me into a yellow sundress from the attic shop and I'm not even in this stupid contest. Me and Mama and Janelle are in the middle school choir room helping Darla to get ready. It smells like hair spray enough to make you gag.

My sister had to keep curlers in her hair all day long plus last night. She tied a scarf around them for the ride here. Janelle's pulled them out and piled all the hair up onto Darla's head with a bunch of stray curls hanging out here and there. She takes a long time to do Darla's face. She opens a box with pencils and powders and all kinds of stuff. It folds out in two directions like a tackle box and has tiny drawers like the shelves I saw in Whitey's workshop. Every time my sister turns to see who's coming in the big double doors, Janelle jerks her chin back under the light. She says Darla's got to be still, damn it.

My mom asks my sister is she ready, and she nods her head.

"How are you going to walk?" asks Janelle.

"Squeeze my butt cheeks together and pull back my shoulders."

Darla looks scared, and it makes me think of how last summer we used to plan to camp out up in the turkey house. Just talking about spending the night in there with the woods behind us and the old animal smells all around us was enough to spook us. We didn't ever need to actually do it.

"Don't touch that too much." Janelle pulls my sister's fingers away from where the curls are fastened like a crown on top of her head. "You're going to make it fall."

We have to kiss the air next to Darla's face so as not to mess anything up. After we leave, I run back real fast and find her pinning a slip of paper onto her hip. It's got a big "12" written on it in black magic marker.

"I forgot to give you something," I say, thrusting the lure into my sister's hand.

"What's this?" She fingers the feathered tail.

"It's just a lucky thing," I say. Then I run like hell to catch up with Mama.

The contest is long and boring and kind of like the Christmas pageant at the Presbyterian Church. The one where they make all the kids come up to the microphone and say a little poem. It's hard to tell all the girls apart when they're up there on the stage. They're all standing the same, and they've got on so much make-up. When Darla steps forward, though, there's something shimmery dangling from her hair.

My sister doesn't win, and after the show everyone tries to stand around and tell her it's okay, that she was definitely the prettiest one anyway. She just wants to know can she please, please go down to the carnival with Shane.

Jed looks over to the corner of the chorus room. There's Shane Spangler standing against the wall, wearing brown pants with the shirt tucked in all tight instead of his red shorts and whistle chain.

"I'm sorry, Sweetie," says Jed. "I just don't think that's a good idea. You can invite him to go on the rides with us on Wednesday."

She walks over to Shane real slow and whispers something in his ear. He nods his head and hugs her, then goes on without her.


That night Darla and I catch fireflies like we used to along the hillside behind our trailer. The grass is all damp with night, and I feel like my bare feet sliding over it must leave a wake in the moonlight. The woods behind us are full of fireflies because it's almost the end of the season. They hang like far off Christmas lights, and every so often the leaves rustle around over our heads. Then I have to look up because it's like they're sighing, "Summer..."

We sit down with our backs against the deck and try to count how many insects are lighting up our jelly jar. Darla's scrubbed her face clean, and now her nose is shiny beneath the porch light. I get a little hurt in my heart then and a feeling like something's about over. Like when Jed and his boss start unloading the boat for the day up at Lake Moomaw.


I'm not sure how much later that same night I hear the window screen pop out in the room next to mine. I rise up and, holding onto to the white iron bars of my daybed, standing in the middle of a twisted pile of Holly Hobby sheets, I can see myself reflected in the mirror. There are tufts of red hair matted against my face, and my nightgown, one of Jed's old T-shirts, has slid way down across my shoulders. My breasts look like little pink moons above my belly. The jar of fireflies is sitting on my dresser. Most of the insects have settled to the bottom, but a few float up every so often, flashing quiet and sending light creeping up my bedroom wall.

The rocks are stirring on the ground outside, and my sister's flip flops slap against the gravel. I know pretty soon I'll hear the engine start in a red truck somewhere down the hill.

## Man with Swatter

On his front porch, on a folding chair.
A scowl governing his face. In his left hand,

a brown beer bottle. The right, the wire
handle and plastic mesh, spotted

with casualties. Little fly guts. Little fly
wings crumpled like cellophane.

The noonday sun hammers the roof
of his house, nails its shadow to the dirt.

When he lifts his left hand, he's quenched.
The right, another fly's erased from the world.

Look closely at the ferociousness
of his swing—the way his scowl, for half

a second, becomes even more deformed,
even more like a jack-o-lantern's—

and you'll understand how a man could kill
another man. Without a thought. One quick

move. The air whistling before his hands
lie still in his pockets like tarantulas.

# Echo

A housewife lifts to her ear her husband's fedora.
Where it swallows his crown she hears the ocean
of his thoughts: *Margaret, oh Margaret, sweet*

*lovely Margaret.* The housewife doesn't know
any Margarets. When she holds his black wingtip
to the side of her head, it's the clack of his footsteps

over sidewalk, a lobby's marble. Carpet muffles it.
Mutes where he's headed. She brings to her ear
the dark opening of one deerskin glove and listens

to the hush of his hand sliding against silk, against
skin. Twilight and the telephone sounds its alarm.
Against her ear the housewife presses the receiver,

her husband nattering on the line. Says, *I'm caught
up at work.* Says, *I'll be home late.* In the cavity
of his voice she hears a reverberation, the words

behind the words. Hangs up and feeds a suitcase
her belongings and latches it shut, a sweater's red
cuff hanging out like a bitten tongue. No letter.

Whatever's to be said the house will say for her.
The front door left open like a mouth in disbelief.
High-back chair pushed away from the dinner table.

A blank notepad on the kitchen counter imprinted
with a grocery list: *trash bags, eggs, sourdough, milk,
cold cuts.* The faintest echo of what they needed.

# The Eyes

Forever our eyes are grabbing.
Be it what a windshield brackets,

be it the television's onslaught:
collie in mid-air snapping hold

onto a Frisbee, a magnified
razor shearing off a black forest

of stubbles, and so on. Then
a wildfire's eating the hills,

a weatherman points to a storm
pinwheeling around an eye

that never blinks. A book,
the eyes love a book, following

every word's inked footprint
from margin to margin.

Museums too, how the eyes
sponge over a Miró or Klee,

the ice cream and bubblegum
hues of a De Kooning. Let's not

forget the movies, a hotspot
for the eyes, so many lifted

from darkness to a screen
illuminated by the car chase,

a bed sheet's heave and fall,
the orange rose of an explosion.

Sometimes the eyes are fooled,
*trompe l'oeil* they call it,

a brick wall that's really a wall
with painted on bricks.

Or the eyes just quit, a shadow
swallows them like a pair of dice

in a velvet bag. Tell me how
she does it, this woman skimming

the sidewalk with a white cane,
eyes sunk behind shades?

In the directory she's mapped
in her mind, it says *You Are Here*

wherever she stands. But where
are we when a benevolent hand

brushes our eyelids closed
for good? Let me start this over:

For now our eyes are grabbing . . .

# Lunch

The Dalton Building was twelve stories high and she worked on the twelfth. Her desk faced a shorter building of red brick, over the top of which she could see the river and beyond the river, Canada. Before she began typing she had to touch the eyes of both eastern bluebirds in the picture on her desk. Sometimes she didn't realize she'd added a phrase like *why is there so much cheese* to the middle of a letter that was not about cheese. When her boss pointed out these intrusions, she stared at her hands and wondered if she was more than one person. The gamma-ray burst source in Leo had just been discovered. She memorized what Krzysztof Stanek had said in *Discover Magazine*: "In just a few seconds, it produced as much energy as our sun would produce in ten billion years." She was eating lunch in the southern stairwell when the man in the ski mask came. She always ate lunch on the landing between the second and third floors because she could see the bronze swans in the fountain from there. The ski mask looked itchy and hot. He pointed a long barrel at the book she was holding in front of her face. It was about the solar system and quarks, about big things made of small things. When she lowered the book, the gun made a noise like it was clearing its throat. She was unsure if this was the safety being moved or a shell slipping into place and wondered how she would look dead. When he noticed she'd peed, he dropped the gun a bit and she lifted half of her pastrami sandwich toward his face. As he walked by, he took the sandwich and she touched the back of his left calf. When the third floor door clicked shut, she ran to the lobby and told the man wearing the shield about the ski mask and gun. The first shots came faintly, tiny pops like soap bubbles bursting, and then screams of various pitch and duration interlaced into a wind rushing from stairwell into the lobby. She walked across the street to be with the swans. Cop cars, ambulances, fire trucks, news vans hived around the building. A man put a microphone in her face and asked how she felt. When she said something about seconds and the sun and ten billion years and a sandwich, he made a slash across his throat and the camera woman turned the lens on a man running from the lobby with his arms spread wide like a crucifix. At home, there was a message on her machine from Sears, a woman asking if she was interested in the extended warranty for her blender. She dialed her mother's number even though her mother had been dead for two years. The man who answered coughed a long while before he could say hello. When she began to cry he said I'm going to hang up now but he didn't.

# Their Days Remember the Bludgeoned Girlfriends

Blood is meant to be unseen
and fail to have a taste. The dream is drenched.
All the late nights talking too much are still
listening and the last rainy day without an umbrella
wishes to come back and rinse them.
The rule is blood stays in, never leaves you,
unless for the fluency of woman.
Gentle is the brain, firm the bone.
All the fields and streets they ran through compel
them with their endlessness: remember how we were
together? Prior and post bat and hammer, jack
and marble mantle, so open-minded, so
easily crushed.

# A Soft Explosion

Only because we didn't hear it, a noise so loud we
should go deaf, we call it soft. A man punches his crying infant
in the chest while his girlfriend smokes a cigarette
on break at work, or something similar everywhere,
the one who gave birth to the one who dies fully trusting
the mercurial fool who seeded her. And the heart explodes,
like the laughter of the women saying, tell me about it,
over some new version of the same old story, and you can't
see the damage in the little package of pastel cotton,
smooth skin, how oceanic the planet of body is, blue all over
the bones, until or if he is opened up and then, scarlet
all over the cage that trapped him. What does it feel like,
do you think, like being inflated? He wasn't trapped, he'd like
to talk back, not yet, he wasn't, he wasn't ready to go free.

# The Zen Adventure of Gerald Riley

My friend Gerald Riley went over the wall, as they say in Zen circles. What that means is, he escaped from a sesshin—a silent meditation retreat. At about one in the morning he opened a window next to his bunk in the monastery Guest House and squeezed out, dropping eight feet to the grass. From there he climbed over a brick wall, kicking and grabbing until he fell on the other side by the sidewalk. Believe me, this was an almost superhuman feat for him. Gerald is fifty-eight and looks it. His waistline has exceeded his inseam for so many years he doesn't even think about dieting anymore. He started walking down the sidewalk, keeping an eye out for a taxi.

Poor Gerald, I thought when I heard about it. I'd gone to a sesshin the year before, and I know how tough they are. You're locked in a monastery for seven days and nights, sitting motionless on a little *zafu* cushion, staring at a blank wall and keeping your mouth shut. They get you up at four in the morning to do that. Once in a while a little man with a shaved head comes along and spanks you sharply on the back with a stick called a *kyosaku* to make sure you're not getting too comfortable. There may be fifty other people in there with you, but the silence makes you feel like you're hiking alone to the North Pole.

Most people get through sesshins all right, and even come away with a little pearl of peace in their hearts, which I guess is the least you should expect from such an ordeal. But others don't hack it.

I didn't think a sesshin was a good idea for Gerald. I'm not talking about his weight. A lot of chubby people go to sesshins and do just fine; some reach enlightenment just like a gaunt person. But Gerald likes his creature comforts, his fresh-ground coffee and newspaper in the morning, some leisure time on the john, and lunch at the Squirrel Hole where he favors a Dubonnet with a steak sandwich. Still, he was determined to go. You see, his ex-wife Elicia—Argentinean, and a beauty—had moved from Pittsburgh to

Georgia just to be near the Savannah River Zen Monastery and join their sesshins whenever they held them for people outside the monastic order—men *and* women—seven times a year. She was making herself over from the inside out. Their marriage had ended, some months before, possibly because Gerald couldn't imagine giving over the dark and dualistic world of business for chanting the sutras. But he still missed her dreadfully, and it choked him up when he heard she was even thinking of becoming a Zen nun. He bought a plane ticket to Atlanta and caught the AAA shuttle to Augusta.

I called him before he left. I said, "Gerry, does Elicia know you're coming?"

He answered, "It's not up to me to tell her I've decided to work on my soul."

But it turned out to be even tougher than he'd imagined. The sesshin started on a Saturday night, and by the next night his knees and hips were on fire from the medieval sitting postures, he was trembling from caffeine and alcohol withdrawals, and tormenting himself by mentally undressing Elicia who sat four cushions away deep in meditation. Nor did she acknowledge him with so much as a twitch of her eyelid when they passed in a hallway on their way to and from visits with the teacher, Isan-Roshi. Elicia carried the rule against speaking even to the far bounds of the figurative.

He'd followed her bliss into hell.

"What did you expect?" I asked him later.

But he just shook his head.

Actually, the escape I started to tell about was his second in as many days. The first was the night before, a Monday, and it went so well that he decided to try it again. That Monday night he'd flagged a taxi and gone straight to Augusta's notorious Broad Street, where there are strip joints about every twenty feet. He went into the Basket of Dollies where he settled his girth into a chair at a huge table on which a nubile woman—Debrina was her name—danced wildly and feathered off what flimsy clothes she wore to start. Seeing the portly bespectacled man with his elbows on the table, she bent over in front of him, shaking her shaved crotch near his nose while simultaneously taunting him with her face between her knees—hissing, running her tongue and gnashing her teeth. She was so close he could hear—even under the rock

145

music—her two cheap metal crosses, on a chain around her neck, dinging faintly as they struck together. Gerald's glasses steamed. Trembling, he tucked a fifty dollar bill under her garter, along with a lot of one-dollar notes the poorer young boys had stuck there. When she saw it, she smiled and kissed his forehead and mussed his hair. Gerald's heart pounded dangerously.

He'd never been to such a place before. Or, so he told me; and I believe him. Completely impulsive and out of his character, it was a reaction to being locked in the monastery, the enforced silence, and the pain of seeing Elicia. Other than in movies, he'd never seen a naked woman before, except Elicia. And even with her—dear God!—he'd never stared eyeball to pussy, which he'd known only by touch.

Getting back into the monastery was another matter. After the taxi dropped him off, he scaled the wall again, bashing his shins. Then, realizing that the Guest House window was an impossible reach, he walked into the shadowy inner yard where he crawled under a spruce tree and sat, resting his back against its trunk. Exhausted, he dozed, got up once or twice to urinate in the Japanese flowers, and slipped back under the tree to sleep. He dreamed himself back in the taxi, pulling up in front of the monastery; but, being too weary to pull the door handle, he rode helplessly away again.

He nodded awake at 4 AM when he saw the senior monk coming down the path from the Main House—in his bare feet and robe—with his big iron bell that sounded like a cowbell. Crouching low, Gerald watched the monk enter the Guest House—as was his regular morning ritual—to jangle the bell outside the door of the women's rooms, then stalk directly through the men's rooms ringing it next to the beds, jarring men upright.

As they stumbled outside like bugs after a fumigation, the monk ordered them into a silent circumambulation around the inner yard, a brisk stride in the chilly morning air to get their blood moving. When the monk was looking in another direction, Gerald left his black street shoes under the tree, and stepped out of the shadows to join the line. His bare feet chafed on the cinder path, and several times he bit down on a curse before it blurted from his lips. Almost diametrically opposite him in the circle was Elicia, thin as a small tree in her robe, hands folded softly against her *rakasu*—a kind of apron over her breast that signified

146

her commitment to the Dharma. She'd begun braiding her dark brown hair in a long rope, which made her seem taller and thinner, and somehow stronger. She used to call him Sugar-Belly, though that part of their past seemed impossible now.

One of the last things she'd ever allowed him to do for her was wash her feet, plagued with plantar warts, not so long ago. He'd massaged her arches and tendons—hard as little cables—and put medicated pads on the warts. She'd flinched then. Later she insisted on washing them herself. Now he wondered how her feet were holding up. Maybe they were as galling as his own; maybe she just didn't show pain like she used to.

The day was brutal. He nodded off on his cushion, taking blow after blow on his back from the monitor with that damned *kyosaku* until he felt a horrible urge to grab it away and beat his head bloody. Late in the morning he nodded off during Isan-Roshi's homily, though he heard parts he found dumbfounding: about a young Zennie—centuries ago—who stood barefoot in snow all night outside a monastery before he was finally accepted in as a student. Why did it all have to be so damned hard? By evening, when the *dokusan* bell rang and he trudged down the dark hallway to get into line to see Isan-Roshi, he felt better, like he'd accumulated enough nods over the day to be almost rested. As if the booze the night before had been good for him.

When his turn came, he entered the *dokusan* room where Isan-Roshi sat on his cushion under the grimacing portrait of an old Japanese Zen master. Or *probably* Japanese. Gerald told me later that, after a while, everyone at the monastery looked Japanese to him, like Isan himself. Maybe it was just the shaved heads, he mused; or the robes and the erect postures; or maybe their features were really changing from eating the pickled vegetables and rice. Or, just his imagination. There were no mirrors available during sesshin, so he couldn't check to see if he was starting to look as Japanese as everyone else. Everyone, that is, except Elicia.

Gerald bowed to the teacher, then did a roly-poly prostration on the floor before settling himself on the cushion in front of Isan.

"Hah, Gerald-san," Isan said, "you have found out what you doing here?"

That question hit Gerald right in the eye-between-his-eyes. This was his sixth or seventh interview with Isan already, but

147

up to now Gerald had asked all the questions. "What am I doing here?" he repeated the question now. "What do you mean, Roshi? I'm sitting in zazen, eating flavorless food, and I've been assigned to scrub the first floor toilets."

Isan-Roshi's smile was so broad he thought the bottom of the man's head might fall off. "Good, Gerald-san. Good, good." And he picked up his hand bell and rang it in the air, signalling the end of their meeting.

Gerald bowed his way backward out of the room. Somehow he didn't feel that his true self had made any strides in that meeting. If anything, it felt more irascible.

---

That night he couldn't sleep again. Three or four of the other men in the room were snoring like wood-chippers. And all he could think of was Elicia: her vagina, her legs, and belly—and her vagina. What if her pussy had been shaved, would it have looked like that little tart Debrina's in the Basket of Dollies? While the others snored and bubbled, he reached for his clothes on the chair next to his bed, pulled them under the covers where he wiggled into them. Lastly, he reached for his shoes, and threw them out the window.

On the sidewalk again, he knew he might have a considerable walk before a taxi came, since it had been a little hard to get back from Broad Street the night before. Only a few cars passed at all now. A black man approached on the sidewalk, carrying a paper bag in his arms, and Gerald stopped him, and asked if he had a car.

The man hesitated, and said, "A car, you say? No, I ain't got no car."

"None at all? None you can use?"

The man stepped under the street light where Gerald could see that he was elderly. He'd thought the man was younger because his step seemed springy.

"My son got a car."

"I'll pay you a lot of money if you'll give me a ride downtown."

The man squinted. "Mister, are you in trouble?"

"I don't know. I may be."

At that moment a large black sedan squealed around the corner and sped toward them. Gerald heard the brakes sing, and as the car pulled to a stop next to them, the side window was already descending. "Gerald-san, get in," said a voice.

Gerald froze to the spot. The black man walked quickly away. The door of the car opened and Isan-Roshi stepped out and held the front passenger door open for him. He was dressed in plain dungarees and an open L. L. Bean jacket; and for the first time, Gerald realized how small his teacher was—his head came barely to the top of the car. "Please," he said a little imploringly.

So, Gerald slid into the front seat. Isan-Roshi got into the back. One of the Roshi's senior students was driving, Harmon Smythe, an Englishman with a shaved head, who had been the one who opened the monastery's big front door when Gerald arrived the previous Saturday. Gerald had noticed then that the lad sniffed his scotch breath (Gerald had asked the shuttle driver to drop him off a couple blocks from the monastery where he went into a bar and downed three double scotches before the sesshin). Now Isan told Harmon to drive back to the monastery.

A robed woman was watching out the front door when they pulled up in front of the Main House. Her name was Vera, a nun. She'd been the second person he'd met there, who had also puckered her nose, but had assigned his number, 38, which identified his bunk, his *zafu*, and was probably the number they'd write on his body-bag if he had a heart attack. Gerald looked at her indignantly as they came in the door, and she turned away, walking ahead to open the door to Isan's office. Somehow everything she did seemed ritualistic to Gerald, even a simple thing like turning a doorknob, and it annoyed him bitterly.

Gerald took a chair. Harmon and Vera stood against the wall with their arms folded as if at any moment they might have to defend their teacher against a physical attack.

"Now," Isan said, seating himself at his desk. "What you doing here?"

At this moment Isan seemed less like a venerable teacher to Gerald than a petty third-world bureaucrat.

"I'm being held against my will," Gerald snarled. "It's a federal offense."

"I do not prevent you from leaving. But I ask why...."

"All right then, I'll be going," Gerald said getting up. "I'll get my stuff out of the Guest House."

"Wait," Isan said, holding up his hand. "You cannot go there at this hour, you will disturb others."

"But I can't leave without my belongings."

"Why not? You did not take them to Basket of Dollies."

The hair stood on Gerald's neck. "How do you know where I went last night? I didn't see you there."

"I have friend drive taxi. Now you tell me what I do *not* know. Why you here?"

Defeatedly, Gerald flopped down in the chair again and told Isan-Roshi the whole sad business—about Elicia, how he'd lost her and had tried to follow her into her new world, but found it inhospitable. Now he was sorry, and felt like a fool. He wept. "But," he added now, glancing quickly from Isan to his two helpers and back again, "I really don't want to leave, I don't want to go home now." Though he wouldn't admit it, he still felt a horrible need to be near Elicia. But also, he was almost half-way through this damned sesshin; and, brutally hard though it was, when he imagined flying home early he saw himself deflated and confused. "I have never been a quitter," he asserted, stiffening himself. Harmon looked bored, like he'd heard this too many times.

"I afraid you must leave," Isan said. "You here for all wrong reasons, Gerald-san."

That was when Gerald, my old friend, threw one of his notorious fits. One of his meltdowns. He doesn't do it often, maybe once every couple years. Elicia must have witnessed more than one. Maybe his fits even contributed to their divorce in a small way. But I've only seen one full-blown performance (at a team-building seminar for the investment firm where we both worked), such as he gave them now. He slammed both fists on Isan's desk, screaming and threatening self-mutilation and suicide; he rolled on the floor beating himself about his head and chest until Harmon and Vera picked him up by the arms and set him collapsed and sobbing back in his chair. Harmon went out and returned with tea on a little tray and gave him a cup. Slowly he regained himself. He sipped—or slurped, rather.

When he finally spoke again, it was like the efforts of a man who had just climbed an exceedingly high ladder, his lungs gasping with something important to say.

"I am prepared," he said, gasping more, "to write a very sizable check to this monastery...to allow me to stay in this sesshin until the end." He choked and took a sip and another deep breath before saying, "But on one condition," as if their acceptance was a foregone conclusion. He waited for someone to ask what that condition was. When no one did, he continued, "I must sleep in a private room."

Isan refused the money, but imposed his own conditions. Gerald was moved to an oak-paneled room in the Main House with a four-posted bed. But, beginning the next morning, he was to scrub all the toilets in all the buildings both upstairs and down—a back-breaking task, more Sisyphean than Herculean since by the time he'd cleaned the last toilet, scrubbing it inside and out, the first was filthy again. To complete it took far more than the regular after-breakfast work hour that was part of the daily routine in sesshin, but also the free hour in the afternoon when most Zennies caught a wink of sleep. Even after the last formal sitting ended at 10 PM, when other Zennies wandered off to bed or to dark corners to continue their meditation into the wee hours, Gerald could be seen running between the Main and Guest Houses with his bucket, brushes and rags. He was beyond weary, on another plane altogether in which his last glimmering electrolytes were being spent. But Gerald was taken now with an almost creepy contentment, focused in a way he hadn't been for years—unless he counted the twenty minutes he'd spent watching Debrina in the Basket of Dollies. At midnight he collapsed in the oak room bed until the clanging of the four-o'clock monk came by his door.

"Let me tell you," he told me later, "that little runt Isan knew what the hell he was doing, sticking me on that toilet detail."

Because, although the long hours of sitting on the hard little *zafu* remained torturous—with the silent and self-absorbed Elicia nearby—he now entered long stretches of exausted meditation in which he was conscious *only of his breath*, inhaling and retreating from his shallow lungs. He was awed by the sound and feel of his breath, its thin tide flowing between his mind and soul. And when he cleaned a toilet, he polished it like a pearl. Work and meditation were becoming integrated, and he wondered what effect it would have on his job as a stock analyst when he returned home. (A new power of focus—it would have to be good, huh?) When the *dokusan* bell rang the second afternoon, Gerald actually ran down the hallway to get in line to see his teacher, anxious to talk about something that had disturbed his exhausted sleep the night before.

In the yellowish light of the *dokusan* room he fell forward to get the prostration done with, and clambered onto the cushion. Odors of cleaning and disinfecting solutions wafted up from under his robe.

"Careless," Isan-Roshi said.

"Huh?"

"Sloppy prostration, Gerald-san."

Gerald apologized and offered to do it again, but the Roshi shook his head impatiently.

"Roshi, let me level with you," Gerald began, closing his eyes for a moment, wrinkling his forehead. "Something very strange happened in my sleep. In my dream, I mean. That is, I think I was sleeping. I dreamed that Debrina, the young woman who I saw dancing in the Basket of Dollies, came into my room and made love to me. It was so real that I worry it might have actually happened."

Isan-Roshi seemed to ponder this for a moment, twisting his lips in thought. "Is *makyo*," he finally said.

"What? *Makyo*?"

"Yes. Happens in early stage of Zen practice. Illusion. Your mind begin spring cleaning. Carry out garbage. See crazy things go by."

"I admit I was delirious, Roshi. But I could even hear her two little crosses ringing together."

"What crosses?" the Roshi wanted to know. And Gerald explained about the crosses on Debrina's necklaces, such as a religious girl would wear.

"Is *makyo*," he assured Gerald again. "Better be *makyo*, Gerald-san." And he chuckled.

But later, when Gerald slipped back to his room in the Main House to get an extra shirt—it was a chilly evening—he noticed one of the staff working on the front door, apparently changing the lock.

---

That night, after he cleaned the twenty toilets, or thirty or forty toilets—he lost count—also unplugging some which were choked with combs and Tampons and purloined food hastily disposed—he collapsed in his bed, immobilized with fatigue. And then he had the same delirious *makyo*, in which Debrina came into his room in the dark, in a blanket which she dropped at his bedside, and pulling away his covers, took her pleasure on him, running her tongue over his face, making him explode inside of her.

*Makyo! Makyo!* Zen was a screwy world in which both ecstasy and abject pain were disavowed as inconsequential. It thrived on contradictions. They taught him a chant, and then told him to forget it. They strove for awakening by depriving themselves of sleep. Isan sent him to open windows in a room where there were none. They talked in riddles of one hand clapping, and, *Does a dog have Buddha nature?* which he seemed to understand only when he was ready to collapse.

He was wakened by the moon, by its round and nearly-full orb which had moved into an upper pane of the window near his bed. It had been a long time since he'd looked at the moon, or even noticed it, while living in the city in a galaxy of artificial light. It astonished him now, and made him emotional. For a moment he wondered if Elicia was looking at it too, then he decided he didn't care. *He* was looking at it now—that was all that mattered. Although it was a little fuzzy. He felt around on the night stand for his glasses but couldn't find them. Maybe it wasn't important if it was fuzzy. In a homily, Isan-Roshi had quoted an old Zen admonishment, *Don't confuse the moon with the finger that points at it.* So, he would not confuse it with his glasses either.

Then came the bell. He could hear it jangling at the Guest House. Jangle-clang. The monk would be back here any minute shaking it at his own door. He decided that for once he would beat that crazy monk to the draw—he would get up now. But when he rolled toward the other side of his bed, he ran into something solid in his sheets, heavy. It grunted and stirred; and then it also heard the bell, and said, "Oh!" and jolted upright in the bed. "Oh!" she cried again. "Oh my God!" Gerald was on his hands and knees now, staring at her. This was no *makyo*, he was certain of that. He heard his ex-wife's two little Zen bells ding together, hanging from her neck, just like the crosses, as she looked frantically around the room in the dark for her clothes.

He called out to her to wait. That it was okay. He didn't mind.

"I don't care what you think, you dolt," she snapped. At last she found her robe in the dark, and pulled it on over her head. "I'll come back for my other clothes later. Okay? Do you hear me?"

He said, yes, he understood, Elicia.

She bolted for the door, calling back, "Why did you have to follow me down here?"

As she threw open the door, he saw her stop short in the glaring hallway light. He could barely see the monk, but he could hear the bell's clatter go silent as if in shock.

They sat more or less together in chairs facing Isan-Roshi's desk. The venerable teacher hadn't arrived yet, but Harmon served them tea, which seemed like an act of sympathy while also giving the occasion an air of Zen officialdom, even while they waited. But Gerald refused the tea. He was even more indignant than he was two nights before when he'd accused Isan of holding him captive. This was undignified, like being dragged to the principal's office; and he was ready to take Isan's head off. But then he saw how distressed Elicia was, how her fingers trembled when she sipped her tea, and he felt tenderly sorry. Yes, he really had imposed himself on her world. He'd made a terrible mistake. He told her he was sorry.

"Oh," she said dismissively, "there's nothing to apologize for."

"But you seem so disconsolate."

She struggled to take another sip. "That is because I am disconsolate."

"That is why I am sorry."

"Well, then, it's up to you if you want to feel that way, but there's no need."

When Isan came in, his face was flushed with annoyance. After all, they had broken one of the primary rules of sesshin at Savannah River Zen Monastery. You are not to sleep with another person. Guests or not. For the duration of the sesshin, you are to be celibate.

"You both," Isan began, "have wasted time. Terrible waste."

Though it was barely sun-up, their belongings were brought to the front door of the Main House where Gerald sat lacing up his shoes, and Elicia looked silently out a window at the street. The taxi arrived just as daylight outlined the magnolia tree in the yard of a nearby house. When the main door swung shut behind them, he heard its new lock snap hard, automatically. They slid into the back seat, and the cabby asked, *Where to?* Gerald started to say the bus terminal (Elicia lived in Madison, maybe an hour away, and the same bus would go on to Atlanta). But she interjected, "I am so hungry." So he said to take them downtown.

"I've been hungry all week," she added. "I just couldn't get enough food."

Gerald was relieved to see it wasn't the same cabby who had taken him to the strip joint earlier in the week, nor the one who brought him back—one of whom had tattled to Isan. He would have been tempted to strike him all over the head and back, like certain old Zen Masters were known to do to bad little students.

They arrived at a cafe just as it was opening, where they ordered a breakfast of eggs and grits, to which Gerald added sausage gravy. He ate hungrily and loudly, guzzling coffee, and watched Elicia pick at the food she'd declared herself so famished for. He thought they needed conversation, so he talked about the house and the new curtains he'd bought since she'd moved out. Actually, the place was a mess, like a movie set for a story of a man struggling with loneliness—half-bags of cookies everywhere, garbage overflowing. His shirts and slacks were clean only because he took them to the dry cleaners, while he bought new socks and undershorts for each day, throwing the dirty veterans into a spare bedroom where a pyramid of linen grew. So he told her only about the new curtains, and a new power-chair that hummed and gave him massages.

Elicia set her fork on the table. "That is so manipulative, Gerald."

"What?" he asked, shocked.

"To tell me about the house at a time like this."

He was stunned. But then he understood: she was right. This wasn't supposed to be happening to them—this eating together, sitting together at a table or doing anything else together, ever again. At the bottom of all their old bickering, somewhere in the tangle of their struggles to explain themselves to each other, was a reason for their failure, sure as there's a worm in the bottom of a tequila bottle. It's there, why explain it?

"What are you going to do?" he asked.

"Do?" she looked up, as if the verb were the name of a stranger thrown in her face.

"Yes. What will you do when you get home? I mean, how are you going to deal with all this?"

She shook her head. "I don't know. I just feel so awfully humiliated."

Outside they were surprised to see the taxi still at the curb where they'd left it. The cabby said he'd had nothing else to do but wait. Now he drove them on to the bus terminal. And as they rode, Gerald noticed the moon still hanging in the brightening sky, faint now, almost like a face in a double-exposed photo. The moon that he'd been so startled and happy to see, was waning again. "Goodbye, moon," he said aloud, not caring what Elicia would think.

At the terminal he got out and helped Elicia with her bag, and he said his farewell.

"You're not taking the bus?" she asked startled.

He shook his head, and he was surprised to see her look of disappointment. No, he told himself firmly, watching her walk to the door of the terminal and disappear inside, I am not getting on that bus. Then he got back in the cab. He sat for a minute, thinking and stroking his chin. Finally, he said, "Take me where I can buy some ice, will you?"

The cab pulled into a gas station, where Gerald bounded inside and came out minutes later with four enormous bags of crushed ice in his arms. When the puzzled cabby got out and picked up one bag that Gerald dropped, he was promised a big tip. "Back to the monastery. Please."

They lugged the bags to the front door of the Main House. Gerald could only hope the four bags would be enough. One by one, he broke them by slamming them against the iron railing, letting the crushed ice spill out on the front stone steps like a little borrowed winter.

"I thought you were going to throw a big party with this ice," the cabby mumbled.

"No party today."

The cabby shrugged.

"You mind getting rid of these for me?" Gerald asked, handing the broken bags to the cabby. Then he thanked the man and gave him two twenties. He waited until the taxi had driven out of sight before he took off his shoes and socks.

Later, Gerald would describe for me the startled look on the face of the monk who opened the door to answer his pounding—to see my old friend standing in the crushed ice, in his bare feet, begging to be admitted.

## Butterfly Ballot

The Swallowtails bunch on Florida's phlox
like pundits to the flame of argument.
They prefer thistle to the Shepherd's-needle
parasol so popular among the Sleepy
Orange. They say if you snap off the umbel
at the base and twirl it between your thumb
and birdfinger the arable weed will seem a wheel
whose turning can lull you from the falconress
cries of the media as their grip slips
on the 2000 election. It's an effect that starts
with a butterfly plashing its wings in Palm Beach
and ends with a circus in D.C. The streets
in Palm Beach, to speak of streets, are flat
as the insect grasses of the Loxahatchee
and marked in a language with two wings. Too bad
the anarchy of language is lost on the Cloudless
Sulphur, Crayola lemon wings with spots
like fallen chads beneath. Imagine the cruel child
of Coriolanus punching those spots out with a twig
and you can understand the call to politics.
The first time the world divides is easy--
mother every time. The left breast for the right-
brained, oranges over apples, and anything
but polyester. In the cold war of puberty
we lose faith in things red, in lips and Christmas,
and the sky's godless blue stays a confusion.
Maybe we take donkeys over elephants
but it's less a question of smell than sound.
But why break a Monarch on a wheel,
or pin one to a cork board with the pale fire
of a novelist. If we lay the ballot down
with the gentler tuck of a mother
we see its thorax is a map of bad

choices: one flits down an oil-slick back
road; the other turns left in right angles,
so that even his circling is square.

# Royal Street Jug Band

The wind down Toulouse loosens
the shirt back of the washboard
musician and carries none
of the heel tap or throaty
moans at issue from a kid
the New Orleans Parish Jail
knocked the wind out of one Sunday.
He stares so far past a crescent
of women bent on the laconic
prospect of dressing him
that he seems to have lost nothing
or sight of the Faubourg Marigny.

Whatever god trips the pilgrims
rounding the cusp of twenty one
from the straight path down Bourbon
stalls too the antiquer eyes
caning through the franco-swamp past
stuffed in the pockets of Royal.
Something softer than metal
they want, a smaller bell, smaller
house, something to sting their thighs,
love like it's a poison
to love, a hat with a bigger dent,
body close to bony, a song
like a spell to sit for.

## The Keeper of Teeth

Very large when you sleep
On the bed of nails
On the straw mat
Without a hut

But she comes
The one who keeps
Your wrist
Who holds a tooth
In a teak box
Carved with fish

You have never
Heard her water
Articulate a rock
Tell you
*Not here, not here*

Why must you hold her bead
And trace the secret vein?

If it's a hammer
Pressed into your ankle
If a rust of moving
And not being alive
If a louse
If a watery
If a hair

You could be reading
Lantern shadow on your wall
Waiting for a bus
But not getting the point

Having your shoe repaired
By the Queen Mother
Or repeating the phrase
*Gold carp* in an abandoned cafe
As you wait for apple cobbler

The keeper of teeth
Knows but won't eat

She refers to you only
With the sound, *Who*
Takes your wrist
To her bed of nails
Strikes the straw
With two terrible sticks

Lays you down to sound
To sleep with a fish
In the pit
Of each aching arm

# Luminous in the Owl's Rib

Lost in the animal, in the thickening wood.
How long has the owl been hissing?

You saw each star in the sky
like moon glint from tiny tops.
Saw the lightning
bug in a dispersal of evening fires
strike a chord of sunlight
you thought lost. Saw one another
through all flicker of sound.

The beginning and ending of the world
in a crooked elm, poised with a mate.
As if food, as if feeding.
Your silk bark self, limb by terrible limb.

Wings folding the world
back into dark resin.
Grease-fat voice.
Bark, growth, or disease
eyeing you, unflinching, from the cavity
of a tree. As if from inside
some great lost fire
taken from you one night while you slept
in a world from which, in secret,
you'd already been removed.

# And Max Jacob

No one knew why they appeared or what they were doing exactly. But inscribed in the underside of the flies' wings was, clearly, *And Max Jacob*.

The ethologist rubbed alcohol into the wound he detected in the wood denied by the beetle in the bar.

A taxidermist drinking a beer scratched a silk swan into his head. Shot craps. Praised the sensual merits of crushed rhinoceros horn.

The hairy cop and corporal swore, in deepest voice, they never knew he was a Jew. And only slept with him because of so few women.

Even Louis Aragon weighed in, denying emphatically that Max was "writing Surrealist" long before others, because he wrote *The Dice Cup* prior to the movement.

Someone praised Apollinaire. Used the word *inventive*.

Another, the one in hose and heels, asked about them both in inches.

Another asked, *Apollo **who?***

A fly drew near, scraping its wing.

Outside, steam fell from the mouth of a horse, chewing a copy of Breton's *Littérature*, a page of which read, "Read Reverdy, Don't Read Jacob."

Through the fog, the moon resembled the yellow star on the chest of not a few.

A *conspiracy of silence? Max said **that?** posed Apollinaire. Isn't that a bit extreme?* His ghost scratched its own silk swan into his cloud-like head, stirred a stick through a mix of shit and straw, searching—he insisted—for remnants of Max.

# At the Grave of Antonio Porchia

Dear Friends,

We are gathered here to ultimately disperse.

His atoms demolished themselves in trying to avoid one another.

Those who live by the aphorism, as did our Brother Antonio, die inside a single sentence.

The spear of his words was a feather that penetrated his tongue and clasped it in metal birds.

If he had been someone who bled, he would not have turned blue every time he ate peacock pie.

And if his mouth were now not sewn shut, the world would have kept opening.

So, he was always salting his dream with black pepper.

So, he accepted the owl as his favorite rib.

He once told his daughter, *Be a good boy now.*

And to the potter's wheel where he daily hunched, *Where is my wife's left hair?*

Always remember that an axiom in the hand is difficult to mold.

Such a carpenter, planing even the lush grain of Buenos Aires, of the pampa of this lovely suffering world.

You and I will surely miss him, but then you and I do not really exist.

We are here today, yes, to help one another grieve, but also—as he would wish—to roll the many sides of words across Antonio's grave, looking for a seven, an eleven.

I tell you, he kept a small rectangular box (he once confessed) inside a circle of light.

# The Urban Mermaid's Ars Poetica

When I first left the city for the sea
I took my lessons from the cod, who
don't swim near cliffs, avoid the murk
below the shark houses, and won't go
near Octopi Beach, where darkness
spills, a bewitching fall

to a down-there where doors wait
like mothers for you to come stumbling
in, late again. I fluttered on one
threshold or another before I dared
dive deep through corridors of cold
and a cruel water wind. At last I tried

a handle slimed sick with waiting
for me to arrive—turned and pushed
and stuck my arm in. Did I think
there'd be a light, a map? No such
luck. I dropped on my scaled belly,
pulled through the muck, startling

at a milky mother smell or a hand
against my back—hair tangling in
what? A rosary, still unblessed? Phone
line long gone dead? Hunter's vest,
chaise lounge, pearl ring. Shit,
I knew that room (and swore I didn't)—

could barely breathe for all the lilies
and smashed glasses. So I grabbed
the foot of some furred thing—
rushed out and up to the blurred
light to see what it was I'd got, and if
I'd live long enough to sing its praises.

# Tattoo

This is my bastard's birthmark
three ravens, leg to talon
this is the locket I kept in the dark
now an indelible totem

three ravens, leg to talon
heads and tails a hubless wheel
now an indelible totem
coat of arms, the family seal

heads and tails a hubless wheel
a right withheld since I was born
coat of arms, the family seal
now tattooed upon my arm

a right withheld since I was born
stranger who kept me in her womb
now tattooed upon my arm
act of contrition, my bruise, my wound

stranger who kept me in her womb
holds onto me and the one I call mother
act of contrition, my bruise, my wound
secret surrender that all of us cover

holds onto me and the one I call mother
who knows my blood isn't so simple
secret surrender that all of us cover
isn't absolved by a prodigal symbol

who knows my blood isn't so simple
as this, the baby I'd kept in the dark
secret surrender that all of us cover
this is my bastard's birthmark

# Something Like Redemption

Jen's doll is devil-bait
and lives on top Jen's
bed, where Jen dresses
her in Girl-Scout
green and a trashy
blonde wig.
"That's to cover her
horns," says Jen.
The skirt doesn't cover
much of anything: magic-
marker tattoo or plastic
hint of pussy. Jen loves
her despite her missing
finger, the way she
lets all that grease
drip down her chin.
The doll is so
forgiving. Just watch
how each time
Jen picks her up
the doll's eyes slap
open, her horns
wiggle like hips,
and that grin,
that grin tartare
keeps grinning.

# Conception

I'm a lady's man and a cherry intact
I'm pulling into the rest stop
    unbuttoning my blouse
I am twelfth-hour whiskers
I am tongue I am breast
I'm pussy throb and neck aflame
I'm zipper and the other zipper
I am steaming all the windows
I'm delirious radio, stockings run amok
I'm finger, hand, a nipple, another
I'm cock, two fingers
I'm cunt and muscle
    again, again
I am salt
I am musk
I am slap-it wet and pubic hair
I am murk and egg and the fish shoving my head in
I am already dividing and multiplying
    oh pious mother, oh charming father.

# A Grasshopper Walks into a Bar

The trick is to pay close attention to that vodka
you're pouring, and lie: Nope, haven't heard
that one. Then grab the OJ, glance out toward
the pool table to see if Phil's watching you

as PJ or Tin-Knocker Sam says, "So, the grasshopper
hops onto the stool . . . ." Linda sees you're on edge.
She's on her fourth pint since 7:15. You like her, start
to wonder if she'll cut herself off when the bartender

in the joke says, "Hey, we've got a drink named after
you!" "One for the road?" asks Linda. You check your
watch. It's only nine o'clock and already the smoke
eater's snapping like a wet towel. Already there's

a line of quarters shining like Mary Mack's buttons
down one side of the pool table's faux mahogany
edge and there's Phil, shouting "Rack 'em!" "One
more," you relent. Sam says he's buying. Sam's

still waiting for his quarters to come up; you were
about to tell the Valley Girl joke but now he's
telling you how Son of Sam worked sheet metal,
too, and sad thing is he thinks he's flirting. It's

Friday and you've got a full bar, three-deep and
every seat taken, the five Miller brothers filling
the corner by the jukebox, singing along to "Take
It Easy" and waving for another round of ponies.

It's Miller they want, what else, and because Richie
didn't fill the cooler last night you've got to run
back to the walk-in for a bottle of Rosie's and a case.
Ed offers to help, as he always does, but you carry

your own behind the bar unless a keg kicks. You
rest a moment in the cooler's forty degrees, your breath
a trail of smoke. The rubber mat's a bit slick. Each time
you come here you're struck by how the cigarette reek

in your hair mixes with the musk in your turtleneck
and it doesn't smell bad. You're reminded of that
short story where the guy stores his dead mother in his
restaurant freezer, remember how Mark kissed you

here the night before his wedding, how his glasses
frosted over, how he tasted like bourbon and fear.
Hauling out that case you know the local boys think
you're tough—you can fake it as well as Linda can

fake she's sober—that is, up to a point. Now Phil's
out by the pool table slinging cusses at some Vassar
boy, something about calling a shot. Phil can never
know about Mark—it was just that once. Shit, he'd

kill you. How many has *he* had so far tonight? You
eye the baseball bat between the trash can and keg
of Michelob, glad the Millers are still bangin' those
bottles, yuckin' it up through Cindy Lauper, waiting

for the next Eagles tune to come up. The boys have
backed you before. They won't mess with Phil—
it's an unspoken fact he's your man—but they can escort
out the college kid if things get worse. You're head's

humming. You're gulping Diet Coke, regretting the line
you did off Cathy's finger in the ladies'. You call
"Goodnight" to Mr. Dugan, hoping a fight doesn't ruin
your shift or your chances for a decent tip from who-

ever wins the table. You watch Mr. D sway in some
unseen wind as he reaches for the door. Thank God
he's walking home. You'll walk home, too, after you
lock up, but that's a jukebox of songs and a stockpile

of jokes from now. That's after the pool table's gone
quiet, like water when kids are through swimming,
after the cues are stowed in the umbrella stand, after
the Miller brothers have harmonized "Desperado."

You'll cash out, slam a shot, pour the tip jar into your
purse, elbow the light switch, turn the key in the door
and set the alarm. You'll step lightly across the parking
lot, past Phil's truck and Phil passed out at the wheel,

knowing he was out here waiting for you. You'd hoped
he'd gone home. He doesn't think you're a tough
girl. He thinks you're his, and you flirt too much
behind that bar. He thinks he knows what love is,

and as soon as he wakes he's gonna come pounding
on your door to prove it. And though like a bad joke
you've heard before, you know what's coming next,
you'll rise from bed, unbolt the door, and let him in.

# 1970

When I got my head stuck between the porch rails
I was six and didn't know enough yet to hate my
body, though I knew a thing or two about smoking

my father's cigars with Patrick Dunn under the pines
behind his house, and puking while my brother
rolled joints and stacked 45s on the record player

in his room. My sister was older—she turned me on
to Carol King and JT; she swore her friends
would die in Vietnam because her peace medallion

was flammable. She tried to teach me to dance
to those records, but I never was graceful—it wasn't
a surprise when I got my head stuck in that railing.

How did they ever get me out? Nixon was president;
Martin Luther King was dead. The whole country
was in a fix, my father said, though he never said

a word about the cigars. His heart was a shooting
star; I thought he could fix everything. My mother
believed she could fix his failing heart with home-

made tomato sauce and a Manhattan on the rocks.
My mother rose with the fish; she was unable to
cry; she put her hand to my father's cheek, then went

back to work. Uncle Frank called her a good German:
*Arbeit Macht Frei*, he said, and she nearly kicked him
in the shins. I loved Uncle Frank, but I don't want to

talk about him. Uncle Frank's dead. But let's say I do
remember how they got my head out of that railing.
It took a crow bar—took what seemed forever

because the adults had their loads on by then. That
night my best friend and I took turns wearing the wig
and high heels: we were knobby-knee glamorous, we

were nothing like our parents. Uncle Frank leaned
in the doorframe as we preened, fluttered, eyed
the dapper men, toasted each other with empty glasses.

## Anniversary

I kept being drawn to images of emptiness.
Or synonyms for "futility." I had a kind of collection,
which meant I must have wanted something after all.
Or that was the struggle.

                  I was thinking about a particular morning
in bed. It was one month exactly since our anniversary.
Then I remembered eating the soft, sweet cheese
wrapped in pastry hidden in our salad, the two of us dressed up
for each other, a celebration we tried all evening
not to ruin. My thesaurus of lack, my pile of consolations
for what we failed to make or had made, then
couldn't keep—I devoted myself to trying to transform
that absence, until at last I saw it was too pure.
And then history remade itself in the image of loss,
and love fell away and left a kind of gash.
What could I do but touch it, since
the doubters were restored to faith that way. No—
not even a gash, just a place where nothing was, where
a building's been knocked down, then cleared away.
Where nothing was, but it was like nothing else.

# Second Language

Ennuis of French class, trying to distinguish
*Quel couleur est le ciel?* from
*Comment t'appelles-tu?* A long-haired
boy is called Michel. We ridicule him

at recess, misinterpreting
again (his silence, the surge
of *something* we feel joining
against him). The recurring

dream years later reversed
our indifference, his shamefacedness:
in a country of indecipherable
street signs (they're in character,

or Greek, or Cyrillic)
we've lost our luggage,
emblem of our bondage
to things. Hardly tragic

but we're frantic, point, outline
in air the missing objects.
The mime's misunderstood. The train
speeds up. Soon it will be time

to wake in terror. And we do,
to find—we've no idea
how we got here—we're fluent, footsore
from standing for so long inside

the room, or field, or house
we always knew had to exist
of shy murmuring in ears, kissed
fingertips accompanied by a phrase

that comes from somewhere . . .
And to find our intonation
nearly accentless, near-
ly natural, so that the loved one

responds, and comes
at our invitation.

# Simile

Like a thing that wants to yield, and having
laid itself down and become infinitesimal,
ceases to matter. Like the dress in the novel,
pale green silk, that she bent over, mending,
while he could not utter the words and so
nattered on. And then the sky, the
blot of cloud like an enormous fuzzy garment laid out
over the Sierra. All these years inside the compulsion
to hurt, to be hurt or have been hurt, I couldn't trace the hurt.
Or traced it without any fear.
Like my childhood misperception
about sex: that it was necessary but
uncomfortable. If I could discard it and inhabit
the discarded part for a while
and thereby be freed. Or chink off
not the "hurt" but the memory of it dislocated
after years working to turn it into
a hamster or kitten tame enough to be
lifted back into its rightful place. If it
could trust me. Or I could find the simile
by which division could be not healed
but made to shimmer. Or lay down
everything except the effort to love.
And having given all that up, to be
not empty but still, a row of garments
in darkness on their hangers or
a landscape occupied nearly wholly
by sky, just a few inches of sand
or dirt at the canvas bottom.

DAVID KIRBY

## Terrible Swift Sword

Finally I get my nerve up to take the #19 bus
all the way to the end of the line to visit Finsbury Park Mosque,
site of the one-year anniversary "celebration"
of the September 11 attacks and the place
where radical Islamists from all over Europe come to plot
the downfall of the West, and it's a typical
sun-sets-at-four London day, and just as I'm thinking,

How will I know where to get off?, the bus jogs onto
St. Thomas Road and there it is, dome on the right, minaret on the left,
both topped by these horrible-looking swords—
no, quarter moons, but still horrible-looking, all pointy
and sinister, moons falling to earth to sever and maim,
not fun moons like the ones in Shakespeare
or "That's Amore." And there's a guy outside resting

his arms on the railing, but one of his arms is not only
just a stump but a badly-stitched one, as though it had been
dressed in the field or, worse, a basement after an accident
in a bomb lab, and I think, Shit, I can't do this, but then
maybe it happened the usual way, i.e., not in war against
the Great Satan that is me and Barbara and the boys
and a bunch of other harmless individuals but, you know. . .

hunting accident. Job-site mishap. Domestic argument
that went a little too far, that sort of thing. Besides,
just over his shoulder, I can see a card rack. Christmas cards!
No, not Christmas cards, but there's definitely a gift shop,
meaning stuff for sale, meaning my money's as good
as anyone else's, so I get up my moxie and enter,
and there's every radical Islamic doodad you'd ever want:

181

Bin Laden tapes and books and posters, a perfume called
"Secret Man," slippers, caps, and three sizes of toenail clippers—
child, adult, and veterinary strength—
as well as books such as Moulana Majazazami's
*Guidance for a Muslim Wife*, which contains advice like
"When a husband calls his wife at night to have relations
with her and she refuses without a valid Shari reason,

she is cursed throughout the night by the angels,"
and a copy of which I buy for Barbara.
There's also a box for clothes to be donated
to the children of Kashmir, which gives me an opening
to talk to the great fat man behind the gift-shop counter
who even gives me a couple of plastic bags
to put the clothes in, but I figure I'm about as likely

to do that as I am to buy those nail clippers
and the "Secret Man" perfume, because (a) do I want
to mark myself as a sightseer or, worse, a snoop
and occasion the reappearance of the guy with
the missing arm and, besides, (b) do I really want
to make a contribution, however small, to the funding
of terrorists?, the answer to both these questions being "no,"

which is also the answer to my third and final question,
which is (c) do I want to turn on CNN some morning
and see a guy in a Yemeni courtroom wearing one
of my Gap shirts? But I have to buy the book, which I do,
and then it's back to central London and my second mission
of the day, which is to find a gym for my colleagues
Joe Donoghue and Sissi Carroll, who will be teaching here

during the spring term, and I've seen ads—
adverts—for Esporta Health Club, which is near
where Joe and Sissi will be living, so I "pop 'round,"
as the English say, and the two Esporta staffers
couldn't be snarkier, couldn't be more disdainful
or willfully obtuse. No, they don't have a brochure.
No, they can't see why I'm enquiring on behalf

of someone other than myself. No, I'll have
to purchase a temporary membership before proceeding.
        No, they can neither explain their fees nor understand
            why I'd want an explanation. Finally,
I observe that what I'm proposing appears to be just a *little*
            too difficult for them and ask if I might possibly
        speak to a supervisor, but, no, they're afraid

        that's not possible, either, so it's back out into
the London cold for me and hard cheese for Joe and Sissi,
        though I'm sure they'll find a health club somewhere,
            and I'm halfway home when I realize, Fuck!
The one-armed guy and the great fat man
            at Finsbury Park Mosque were nicer to me than
        the two toffee-nosed narcissists at Esporta Health Club!

        Fuck! Ever want to pull your clothes off
and just start screaming? Sure, you'd be arrested, but at least
        things would make sense for a couple of minutes.
            I feel as though steam's about to start leaking out
the side of my neck when I notice that the marquee
            in front of Metropolitan Community Church advertises
        a noon meditation, so I stop in and ask the nice lady

        if the meditation is non-sectarian, and she says yes,
it's like yoga, only "without the plinky-plonky music."
        So I pretzel up my legs and begin to follow
            the nice lady's gentle directives, and, sure enough,
it doesn't take long for my fury to not only abate
            but turn into something like calm, even serenity, say,
        though from time to time there are fits of coughing

        like mortar fire, and when I open one eye,
I notice most of my fellow devotees look as though
        they spent the night on a steam grate and are probably here
            more for the free doughnuts than the spirituality,
but I hang in there, and, sure enough,
            my black-and-white world view begins to break up
        into a scattering of lovely grays as I recall the story

Willie Nelson tells about a guy named
Ben Dorsey who used to work for Johnny Cash,
        and he had a bunch of suits that Johnny had given him,
        and one day Ben was walking down the street
in front of the Grand Ole Opry, and this guy
        comes up with a guitar in his hand and thinks Ben
        is one of the stars because of the fancy suit,

        so the guy says, "How do you get started
in this business?" and Ben says, "Ain't but
        one way, hoss. You start at the bottom,
        you go right to the top. Don't mess
with that in-between shit."And, sure, it'd be nice
        if things worked that way, as they do in most movies,
        even *The Dancer Upstairs*, which I'd seen

        the night before near Leicester Square
and about which director John Malkovich
        says, "The movie says that good follows good
        and bad follows bad. Now, I don't believe that.
But I think the world wants to believe that,
        and that it's best to believe that. If you don't think
        that way, everything gets a little too complicated."

        Ah, London: I've lived in you four months,
and I still don't know which way to look
        when I cross your streets. One night
        I see Harold Pinter in a pub, and the next day
I read that producer Sam Spiegel once told Pinter
        "The secret of happiness is whores."
        Maybe. Probably not for the whores, though.

        During the Monica Lewinsky scandal,
my mother-in-law visits us in France,
        and when I say the French aren't as upset
        about it as a lot of Americans seem to be,
she says, "Yeah, well, it's a way of life for them, isn't it?"
        though I can't tell whether she means lying,
        oral sex, lying about oral sex, or all three.

When the meditation session is over,
the nice lady offers us a cup of tea,
    and a man wearing three overcoats motions me
        into a corner and says, "May I tell you
a joke for a tiny piece of change?" I'm so happy
        I could kiss him. They're okay by me, the English,
    even if we don't speak the same language.

# Letter Home on My Birthday, November 29, 2002

*A painting in a museum probably hears more foolish remarks than anything else in the world.*
                        —Edmond and Jules de Goncourt


Well, that painting never rode with me on a London bus!
    What rubbish the English spout, especially when
they're shouting into what they call their "mo-biles."
    "Hullo," says the woman in front of me, "hullo, hullo!
        I say, don't shout! Hullo?" And then one chap wishes another

an 'Appy Thanksgiving, and at first I think, Thanksgiving?
    and then sure, why not, we already sold them Hallowe'en,
and we *did* rid them of a bunch of pesky Puritans,
    so why not turkey, cranberry sauce, and sweet potatoes,
        with or without the little burned marshmallows on top?

Or maybe I just heard wrong: every schoolchild thinks
    that the dying Lord Nelson said "Kiss me, Hardy"
as he lay mortally wounded on the quarter deck of HMS *Victory*,
    whereas what he really said was "Kismet, Hardy,"
        as in Fate, Destiny, All She Wrote, The Big Casino,

Our Records Show Your Policy Has Lapsed, Mr. Nelson.
    Or maybe I heard right but didn't understand:
the night before, we go to the Royal Albert Hall to see the whirling dervishes,
    white-skirted mystics spinning in praise of Allah,
        but even though the MC says it's a religious ceremony

and we shouldn't applaud, we good liberal Westerners can't help
    but show our resounding approval of the Sufi masters,
which means half the audience cheers as lustily as though
    the local lads are winning the test match as the other half
        tries vainly to silence them... So many... *phenomena*!

So little wisdom. After Thanksgiving, the second big celebration
      in November is founded on the historical truth that,
in a little manger outside Baton Rouge, Louisiana, a child was born
      who happens to be your present hero. So today we are felicitating
        this avatar of all things fungible, not to say nugatory,

in the human spirit by going to Bates' Gentlemen's Hatters
      Since 1783 in Jermyn Street to buy him a stylish lid.
It's a narrow store: nothing but hats, floor to ceiling, and not those
      look-at-me-'cause-I'm-a-fucking-idiot Crocodile Dundee-type affairs,
        either, but real hats, stylish numbers your Cary Grant

or your Gary Cooper would be tickled pink in.
      Out of the darkness scuttles this diminutive being who instantly
figures me for a "soize fifty-noine," and within minutes
      I emerge sporting a gray felt trilby, wondering if the gnome
        were Bates himself, not only undiminished by 219 years

of indoor living but unerring in his assessment of cranial diameters.
      But then we go to the British Museum to see
the Piranesi prints; on our way out , the guy behind me vuh-vuh-vuh—
      BLOOOORCH!—he vomits all over me! Barbara drags me
        into the Baby Changing Room to towel me off as best she can,

and I'm telling you, reader, even the babies don't like it very much!
      They throw their fat legs in the air and howl, not that they smell
all that great to me. Also, I'm sure you'll believe me when I say
      I have my choice of any seat I want on the #19 bus back to Islington!
        So you now know it's not all gray felt trilbies over here.

That night we dine at Lindsay House in Romilly Street,
      and when I order the grouse, the maître d' leans over and tells me
solemnly he's afraid they are "shot grouse, sir" and for a moment
      I don't take his meaning, but when I do, I beam at him speechlessly
        and then blurt, "You are, like, so excellent!"and, sure enough,

soon find myself spitting out the little lead pellets with a buh-ding!
    and thinking how brutal that the grouse are slain at the apogee
of their flight from earth, poor dears, but then, just as quickly,
    how happy it is that they are not only blind to the barrel
        that's pointed their way but deaf as well to the annihilating bang,

and also how less than fortunate are so many of we the human,
    subject as we are to every variety of disorder both infectious
and degenerative, with no guarantees that our medicos will be
    any more skilled than 19th-century frontier surgeon Robert Liston,
        soi-disant fastest saw in the west, his record being the procedure

during which he amputated the leg of his patient (who died
    of gangrene), sliced off the fingers of his assistant (who also
died of gangrene), and severed the coattails of a spectator
    (who died from fright on the spot), thus completing in under
        two-and-half minutes the only operation in medical history

with a mortality rate of 300 per cent! Oh, well, say the theists,
    it's not so bad, this way you get to see The Redeemer
that much sooner, no waiting, nosiree. Yeah, that'd be okay
    if God turned out to be as benign as He is in the storybooks,
        but what about what Heine said? Heine said, "There is a God,

and his name is Aristophanes." What if God were a lot more
    interested in playwrighting than in making sure we had
a big fat cushion to sit on throughout Eternity? Buh-ding!
    How fortunate are the birds of the air not to be caged in a pen
        but to soar into the dying sun, the only way to go.

## Standing Room Only

With the latest brand of legerdemain,
I bask in the whiteness of your lie.
Immortal dog that walks around the moon,
*These* are the constellations,

The luffing crusts of things beneath shell-shocked grass,
Our plangent staring into the oasis of space.
An hour stands liberated from its sand,
Imbibes a well-stocked cabinet and staggers on,

A voluptuous message in a stained glass horse.
And the religion books smell like bananas
While a Strawberry smell recedes.
A voice trails off,

"Say, that gila monsta ain't no monsta . . ."
But the alphabet mutates in an even weaker voice,
The torn taste of a bedspread on a deathbed,
While a primer of what is known

Floats toward you on a velvet river.
Can you see it? Here, these binoculars should help.
Go on, transgress the marriage to the ear:
A parody of nakedness, Bodhidharma on a raft.

# A Weird Excursion

I know your landscape's inner breezes
More than I know your poems are like a trail,
Breadcrumbs falling from each stanza.
And the rudderless boat that makes us

Vicariously alive steers us into disappearance,
Not perfectly, but what the hell,
I don't want an afterlife with chicken wings
And Bloody Marys anyway. Perhaps

I am an inventor with smashed glasses
Looking out on a farm, marveling
At the dented cows, pissing into a dented
Pail of milk. I wonder, are you

The papier-mâché devils in your book?
Or are you caught in the karmic freeze
Of complaining blithely of some hideous
Revenge to a dusty upside down cross?

Though your poetry reading was splendid,
Time ticked out of sequence that day
And no one noticed, except for a basset
Hound that howled into its water bowl.

And me, I noticed, but I didn't howl,
Not one little bit.

# Homage to Another Young Poet

You thread beauty like a long night-flame
Through the inside corners of my eyes,
And I am charred to a leaf still blazing
Across the stinging November skies

With all the patrilineal grace of a griffin
Gnawing at the splintery edge of what the mind
Leaves out when it would like to know but can't,
Just can't. And in this elegiac wind, I find

That what is left of me would fill a stadium
Of aporias, no, a century, where fingers cross
And uncross in restless prayer and dance
Up and down the tattered keys of loss

Which has been bequeathed to us and it's bottomless.
Take it, you rave, take all of it: flame, prayer,
Griffin, night, loss, prayer, keys, grace—your own eyes
A flickering of lakewater fire.

Because after your offerings of passion and rain,
The air unscrolls before me like a plague,
And maybe I will uncurl myself before some fireplace
And transmute by whispers into the alchemical ague

That I have allowed the alloy of my body to become
Of late. And if I can dissolve still,
Into that air where no human voice returns,
Perhaps I would understand what anneals a will

Past breaking into a trillion-odd shards,
Each engraved with a letter or a word
From a far-off language no one else seems cursed to speak
(And what about the daughters they've destroyed?

Electra falls and falls across Cassandra's
Heavy-breathing bones . . .) No, I'm afraid
That for me, there is no cure: Even tottering Atreus
Could not fall until all the prophesies were made.

But you, my ageless comet,
May your words stream wild like fiery ginger
Across the soiled sky and take root in the night,
Hesperian, that seals you to an age's harbinger.

# Gypsy Summer

There is a votive X tattered like a chewed card,
A duck swaying in the rainless morning on a lake.
And in the brain-balancing streaks of moonlight,
A trapeze crumples to the floor,
Long or oblong, a kind of addition.
I am looking at my credit

Report, bad, very bad credit
I have. I held about 12 cards
At once "for an emergency," 25 years old, rolling the dead gray
    sheets of addition.
I was living in a lacustrine
City, camping out at night on the green floor,
Dreaming of tiny alligators in the moonlight

On a serial killer campus, how the moonlight
Flecked a victim's hair as her head spun on a turn table, a credit
To Danny Rollins' sick imagination, how he wept on the floor
After stealing her student I.D. card
From her headless pocket. The owls on the lake
Were silent that night, in addition

To puffing into phantom letters on N.Y. Times want ads
In my sleep. The moonlight
Came and went, but still I spoke in the vocabulary of lack
When I told the Brooklyn gypsy three months later of my
    spanking credit
And how, if she removed my god-awful curse, I would renounce
    reading tarot cards
for good. She smiled, made me lie down on her polished wood
    floor,

And danced around me counter-clockwise, flooring
Me with her predictions of my imminent demise, in addition
To her prediction of me as a wild card
Who, for $45,000, would prevent all my friends' souls from
    dispersing in the moonlit

Night forever and forever. I gave it to her. People wonder how
    the credit-
Ratings of manic-depressives get so fucked up, and I can tell you,
    it doesn't take a lake

Around a temple of proverbs to tell the tale, no lake
Of infernal fire to help the story along, although the fluorescent
Gates of hell are far from strangers. The false nodes of that
    summer don't discredit
The season five years later, where, added
To my thinking the future mayor of N.Y. was the antichrist with
    a plan, the moonless
Midnight spoke to me in tongues and the bloated transparency of
    angels carded

Me for liquor I tried to buy on credit but couldn't. The addition
Of ducks to the lake in Central Park failed to floor
Me like the Bellevue Moonlight. It bleated, pick a card, any card,
    any card but this card.

# From a Notebook

Here's a theory on vileness, there's its concordance:
an old friend's name is in it, misspelled.
Time is willing, but why let time rule?

Like a kennel for your pet,
but where are the recalcitrant keepers hiding?

A ball was in the weeds
we walked beside, a voice on someone's radio,
another voice, letting you take your time,
and the hollow voice of my sauntering
headlong, and our mutual voice
of antipathy toward X.

It's either shivering or bliss in America,
so many vowels, moans in this language,
picturesque sunset for a week then back home.

I admire the look of anguish on some faces,
decisions by candlelight, lukewarm bathwater.

—But what good are they anyway,
our phobias won't keep us warm tonight?

Still *in medias res* and no god or devil yet?

An awkward nymph falls in love
with a treacherous vagabond.
It's the same old themes: journey,
murder to create.

The conductor listened to his passenger cough
(every twelve seconds in another era).

Having never grown into the logic of our bodies,
we touch each other with child's hands, supine.

Remember exaltation and hobbies?
We collected everything, we delivered
bouquets. In all my life, staring
as I do at walls and in mirrors,
I remember the patches on your coat,
I remember your mother, shrugging.

*Ingratiate, unfold, demand, commiserate, surrender . . .*

"You told us we should sing. We have decided
to moan," said William Stafford.

How to exorcise these silent-stops?
The skeleton is the mind, etc.
You will go to the fire to the great beyond.
Not what we think you are but what you
know yourself to be.

We have been teaching an old, bitter man
to love the butterflies he catches.
First, we taught him that they mean nothing,
next that meaning is not even secondary.

Not the midnight-seeming the church bells
whisper forth. Many children
are hiding (their frail weeping) (and plenitude, too).

"Two loves I have, of comfort and despair,"
said Shakespeare.

What is it about this weather that keeps her still?
Bare landscape—her thoughts—crows in their
disheveled V, formation of the century all over again—
and now you have a link to the grave.

—The radio's still on: *lullaby, talcum, transport.*

In Belgrade you can hear the church bells (March
1999); every collision is a resurrection.

Skin chapped and a recurring memory of sacristy
water in the marble fount, dreadful old sponge.

The wind this morning was like the old
metaphors, soft and unwrapped and keen.

"It's not repetition," said Stein, "it is *insistence*."

—I wrote you a poem, one you could share
with a friend, break off a corner,
your crisp cups afloat in their buoyant saucers.

What season
    sermon
    system?

Within this seeming disaster: I am a tired robot
with wings (as part of the planned design).

## Untitled

Because I cannot touch you
I touch you

in the aluminum daydream,
and safely in this vacancy

I fit the feeling slowly.

Everything is where it is
supposed to be. I could
forget a lot of things—

in the sharp white
amphibian sunlight

the rain against your face
breaks
into a thousand pieces of smile

a thousand episodes of silence.

Somewhere in there
answers are true and
somewhere beautiful.

Things have been better
and will never be this good again.

In the meantime
I lean mine
on the true side
                    and lie.

Anecdotal I: imagine me

a speck in the wind set down—
the nothing of another lovely
evening—on a broken blue chair.

# Untitled

The phone rings and. Today is deflated.
The walls fall round your eyes and I am
                                    nervous

that you no longer, never did
and kicked through every after. The end.

This is the way the hippopotamus moves.
                    Like a bruise.

# Untitled

Now is the revenge     shifting in the high above     the moment
enormous with silence     without you     the atmosphere agitates
insignificance how lovely     end of sentence.

According to the streetlights     I am here to hold     a bouquet
of wilt     in winter showers.     Drizzle the petals softly.

Up in the far apartment     apart from completely defenseless
today you were unmade     and stayed away from the understand.
The silverware the sock drawer     the lights they     turn on

the lights they turn off     a window opens     and a curtain
softens your attention.     Learn the feeling     say a bubble

filled with a fear or knowing     today it could have gone either way.
Hello the face goodbye the eyes.     Welcome back.     I will miss you.

## Darkness

> *"...light is come into the world, and men loved darkness rather than light...."*


*There has to be something said about the darkness,*
*the way it hides in pockets,*
*among lint and forgotten dimes.  It waits*

*for twilight, the first signs of a friend*
*walking toward you; craving a way out*

it settles in
the kiss that changes everything.

# The Blue Fairy

*If you love me, you will come back, alive as before...*
*—Pinocchio, crying over the grave of the Blue Fairy*

I am not really the Blue Fairy
so it doesn't matter whether you leave;
I won't die of loneliness without you here.
And even if I am her,
and even if I do die a little,
we've both read the story,
we both know how it ends:

> You come back
> crying, and so do I.
> And the Blue Fairy becomes a woman
> instead of a forlorn little girl.

Sin and Redemption.

Death and Resurrection.

Distance and Proximity.

These have become so beautifully blurred—

> Like the way you thought
> my tattoo resembled a butterfly;
> you could see the curve of a wing
> when you first looked at it
> without your glasses on.

# True Believer

*What father will open his chapel for our sins?*

Think about how women reached for Him
on the road to Calvary,
in the garden that morning;
how is this different?

A new faith whispers:
We do not need to confess.
lie bare before any altar.
ask a man to unite
what can only be separated by gods.

There will be no trumpet
to call us away from this.

## Island

Only this story of sea, of stone
warming into blue water, staged summer.
In these tropical dreamscapes turquoise reigns,
and over-ripe fruit plays a central role.
No explanations. The sun knows to swell,
to resemble an uncrated orange,
but when will the talking parrots appear?
Palms loll in their lazy windmill way;
of course the couple strolls along the shore.
The sky has no seam, nothing to catch
and unravel, a blue without answers or intent.
She can't find her mother's camera; he misses
the idea of her body, this girl with longish hair.
Bats and crickets pick apart the dark
and in the poufed sea-grass, lizards report
the rain's hesitation.  On the hotel phone
her mother also dreamt polar bears, water
covering the kitchen floor.  Dark rums
and aloes trailing potted arms past sills,
the sun must stain these houses pink and chalky
as souvenir conch and oyster shells.
The Gulf Stream runs into ocean, flatters
the Atlantic's chill, a blue long past
December, the spring blue of sapphires.
Does the sun also love losing itself,
this falling away, the muscled taste of salt?
That night raccoons scale the cypress trees,
olive-pit eyes, too many to count, hundreds
spilling teeth and smoke in silent hoods by the road;
their char and singed fur seem unsouthern,
hunched with cold. They wear their dark rings
indecipherably as Saturn while Jupiter ripples
and sports its red storm. Far overhead,

the smallest major moon of Uranus has broken
over and again. Miranda, a surface past battered,
stone blasted and burned, running like water
until the fragments fall back together inside out
and her core drifts outwards, exposed
in the burgeoning, pin-drop silence of space.

# February

Snow stopped and fell; the day cracked with cold.
A lilt in her voice like the sea, or wild blueberries.
We watched her pour tea, and frost sugar cookies
into angels.  Once I was scarlet, once I was stained.
I knew she was sick; why hadn't I prayed,
or lit the white candles or stacked Hail Marys?
Her house was quiet; end-tables wore doilies.
Outside the neat trellis, her peach trees swayed,
and in the gold-rose dayroom I didn't know
birthday cake could be pineapple, lemon
or made from carrots.  Her eyes turned yellow.
We couldn't see her, Great Aunt Irene,
who brought us china dolls and satin hair bows.
Mornings like wood sparrows. *For ever and ever. Amen.*

After school and nearly dark. Two girls,
quiet voices, Mother's nails down to the quick,
our scratchy uniforms, the sun whirled,
teetering on its noisy wick.
My mother wouldn't. She didn't forget.
She just couldn't leave. Wrens fussed off the bones
of rose bushes.  Our aunt's eyes were violet
but she never married. That night, no moon,
only stars: insipid threats.  We cursed
with red vigor into the coming iris
then someone called.  Some night-helper or nurse.
Irene ate brulée.  Irene ate couscous. Tight-spun Paris,
the streets nearly burned her.  In a cut glass bowl,
one dozen small suns blister and knuckle.

My uncle's wife arrived, a dog bayed
at nothing we could see.  Car windows fogged, buttons
flying, we were fighting our hair out of french braids
in our swampy station wagon.
We were not good children; we could not wait
quietly, hands folded, in our car, for death.
There was nothing, no words for that weight.

The lot's trees were vacant, the grass without breath.
I could not stop thinking of sea gulls, the taste
of old silver and licorice in the air.
Irene all alone. Pink cheeks. A doll's waist.
Her lacy hats. She rode all the rides at the fair
and danced the Charleston, organza whirls in 4/4
weeknights in her mother's heavy parlor.

## White Behaves Generously Despite Its Stately, Unmeddlesome Properties.

Some boys minded red hair. One kissed me
on the ladder. I knew there were birds,

a snake digesting a frog on the front walk,
so we couldn't get inside. The air stopped

breathing. The sun high but cold.
A german shepherd bit a pretty girl's cheek.

Men with guns in and out of bushes.
At times hurricanes. My mind went

away. The twins picking sage
and foxglove. Lost chair cushions.

I counted eight dead crickets.
There was a code to it all, a secret

I heard the first night. Beware the ocean
at dawn. A duck dressed as a baby.

The plaid-suited clown sniffling.
The moon yawned preciously.

Someone's small tongue in the road.

# Like Water

She fell. A muster of peacocks, waving
night's handkerchiefs, petalled and explicit.
She was not pawing the darkness, she craved an end,
the long iris-mouthed rush. No returns. This brick
of quiet. The city air opened; she called at last
to the undertow's velvet, and I think of you there
in your warlock shoes, this hour of falling glass.

I try afternoons, a bookstore on a corner. I talk to you
through telephone wires; abalones unbutton
on other shores. Not a cry, you tell me,
not some circus stunt to raise sawdust.
On the docks men lift the last mossy and armored lobsters
from their wooden traps; a teacher writes her name
inside a mathbook. Years ago at my window, you saw,

I could kick and sniff the same dark.
Despite all this beating, the blue oven sky wanders
over the day's disorder: phone calls and keys
lilypond after you. You did not know her.
There in your armoire, half a dozen Mays.
Air treading glass. Dry thunderstorms again.
The sandpipers never land here. Rain, other colors

she or I could touch. The lack of sea clearly strangles.
How to break like water. No. The dark.
Not time or its rodent clock. No one's breath
or heart in ashes. She fell all night,
gigantic with sky. What about you on a Sunday?
You want to feed the lounge-chair spiders. You press
around me, grapefruit-voiced though absent.

What bothers you most? Evening does not move.
The moon exists to destroy, to mother you
into this silence. Even now the room swirls with autumn,
leaves taking over, August seaweed returns;
I remember rising, the light on my door. Do you not hear me?
The Atlantic spreads its ferns red and cold.
Another struggle underwater. Let go.

## County Airstrip

*How long in that same fit I lay I have not to declare.*
*—Samuel Taylor Coleridge*


Below, the world is reduced
like a stable set,
horses molded the size
of a half dollar,
and the ground tended,
shorn, a man waking
at dawn to watch over
hedgerows and fields
so perfect there must be
nothing to fear.
A Cessna's light weight
allows it to glide to safety
in case the engine fails,
air lifting the plane
as if on strings.

There is a river
and it has no sound at all.

The child dreams
deep blue wallpaper.
In it, birds in a marsh,
layer upon layer of color
so steeped around them they
will never have to leave.
I keep on telling this story,
can't get rid of it
no matter what.
Last weekend I drove
by my mother's house,

and it was okay.
I saw it was a fine house,
meaning it will last,
meaning there is something
left after all.

# Luminescence

Tonight the stars are above cloud, invisible.
They are the brightness under ocean water.
If it were not for what I have been kept from saying,
I would have no words, the darkness coming out of me
like oil as it does out of Stephen who paces
the oriental over and over, paces around
our mother pretending not to notice.

I know this doesn't work.
I know I cannot invent some other truth.
The ocean holds living creatures too frightening
to face: the eel and flat, fast skate.
The ocean also has its own stars
when the light is right.
The ocean's stars are green.

# The Flat Track

The summer wheat shone purple,
green darners cruised over puddles where,
since June, algae grew in a spreading mosaic
and the girl was convincing.
She'd wanted all summer to breeze
one of the horses, even having smelled it:
dark sweat on her palms where she'd hold
the neck tight, loving the horse.
All summer she'd leaned against the tarred
rails and watched another rider,
afternoon sun hot on her back.
At last, late August,
they put her on the bay mare
and led her across the narrow pasture
whitened with seed-blown dandelion
toward the raked training track, one mile around.

What she didn't know was how,
at this gait, a thoroughbred won't be pulled back
and to tighten the reins only pushes
the horse even further out of control.
The girl must have felt a long time pass
and the horse still running, speed below her
on the ground as the hooves blurred together like oil.
She must have stopped counting how many times
around, how many times past the gate where
stable hands stood with blankets to throw at the hooves
until, finally, the mare ran herself lame.

You can tell me otherwise, but it is not until winter
that your shadow will lengthen behind you,
that the angled light will bless your house,
falling at noon on the bright, blue rug.

# Bottom of the Ocean

I want her to draw me a tall
house on a hill, or a kitchen
table, something solid
that can bear its own weight.

At night, after I'm in bed,
she goes to check the bees, lifting
the outer lid to watch them
asleep in their box beside the orchard.

So hot this May,
all afternoon the workers
have fanned their wings,
keeping the wax from melting.

Putting her face close
she smells the dim honey,
dreams she is young again,
in Berlin after the war.

The bees have become
so still she forgets
they are there, invisible
as kelp on the ocean floor.

In the morning when I ask her
for a rabbit, she draws on
from behind so we are looking
out at the exact same world.

# Daylight Savings Time

Starting in late February my mother
would cut the weather page
out of the newspaper
and put it on the refrigerator
as a sign of hope: each day
a minute or two more light.

But it's autumn now.
This week the time changed,
and it's dark by six.
*Think of it as temporary,* I tell myself:
an alcove or loft, place
for waiting out of harm's way.

I take my daughter to dinner.
as we sit behind the plate glass
of Shoney's, the parking lot grows
appalling at the farthest edges.

## Tracks in the Water

The wind chimes are gone again,
and the tracks in the water-logged yard
point to the home of
the student nurse.
That woman is screwing with
my Feng Shui.
Those tinkling bells
are my ancestors
trying to tell me something.
I can't help that it's the end
of the month,
and the student
who says she's in the
early stages of death
has run out of Ritalin
which she doesn't need
but takes to enhance her focus.
I can't help
that the pencil-thin chimes
sound to her like gongs.
What I can do
is wait out this week
of finals,
avoid that woman who practices
drawing blood,
and try to break
the entangling habit of place.

# No Passengers

She uses black ink
for making triangles and lists,
a figure-eight and an airplane.
She draws responses, draws you into
fist fights, draws conclusions.
She draws ducks.

You hear her say
out loud and firm,
*Mother, we have no goddamn basements*
*in Louisiana. Get it?*
And hit the newspaper
guy's station wagon with
an egg roll.

She draws you out of the picture,
then back in, then out.
She has a schedule of events
she keeps to herself.

And late at night
she wakes to draw self-portraits,
and hides them by the stereo
where it's dark.

# Sometimes We Get So Close

The night you buried
your poems
and married money,
a star deserted the sky
and landed in my
rum & coke.

True the moon
still smiles on
planned communities,
but can you buy the quiet
to build constellations.
Anyway, you choose your poison,

and the subdivision needs
a garden of the month.

## Getting Serious

The glass flashes back
the gray unshaven face
of failure, not, he thinks,
worth the trouble.

In bad times (like now)
he imagines redeeming
whole flea markets
or ruined churches.

And once a girl at a balcony
beckoned to him, but she,
it seems, had merely mistaken
him for himself.

# Confession

bells break
the white silence
of Santorini's
unbearable
shadowless sun
low overhead.
A passerby
fanning himself
with a newspaper
pushes open
the door of the thick-
walled little church
expecting—what?
Receiving only
a cool dark


lit by candles
and a bearded priest
slowly approaching

# Winter Retrospect at the Café Solo

The small bird
in her slender throat
now begins to sing,
a music just beyond
itself as we lean
forward, drinks
lifted.

Now we recall
a smoky gold October
adrift in a sea
of leaves and how
we got from there
to here, almost
safely.

It's a little room
only big enough
to contain
the usual sorrows
and one young couple,
eyes shut, dancing
slowly.

# The Words That Should Have Been Written

Near to the time of your death weren't written then; I was too young
to write them. The tomatoes on the sill, lumpy, irregular,
grown in the yard of the trailer. The fish nailed to a board
to hold it still for you to scale. The picture of you scaling the fish
I developed later, or your father did and it was sent to me;
practical details are unclear.
The jeans hanging low around your hips, belted.
The same belt you would have slipped from its loops years before
if I had misbehaved. The tree with rough pale bark
and small diamond-shaped leaves, the leaves light and dark green,
with spots on them from caterpillars or August blight.
The sandy soil bare in the patch between the two trees,
small orange and brown round stones cresting the surface.
Bowls of them on the sill for me, clear glass through which to look
as the color changed to gold and red in water.
The soil and rocks and trees in general, having been there
every time I visited. The tomatoes just the one time, the last.
I am no longer reminded, exactly. It takes no mention of fishing,
or homegrown tomatoes, or fathers either here or gone.
I see I look just like you every morning.
Every morning, you and your absence both.

# Visit (Preserves)

For a moment in the kitchen
with my mother, cleaning up the canning things,
I understand what marriage might be like
if it were good and lasted.
It's chilly out. When we finish putting jars in stacks
on the pantry shelves, we'll sit in the living room
and read until it's time for bed.
Imagine love lived as though one
were in the middle of it,
as though the middle were other
than the single point at which the funnel tightened
and time's slide turned to a pour
out of our hands toward the long-feared end.
No one I know has gone by tablespoons,
time adding up to something
instead of lost. It must be possible--
that smooth accumulation of days
so familiar from childhood,
slow unspooling of evenings in the garden
or the orchard. Any single one,
this one, held up to the light appears
amber-colored and luminously steady,
collected, kept by the clear glass
of the weather outside the windows.

## Open Mic

We didn't come Mondays for beauty,
though I might not have put it that way then.
We came because it made us feel a little better:
the high school math teacher who sighed like Kenny Rogers
and who, six fingers of Wild Turkey later,
slurred his wife's lies in Japanese,
the parole officer who tossed his motorcycle helmet about
like a headhunter's trophy, the accountant
who bottom-lined all stories into seven algorithms,
then coded his computer to write them.
And me, who'd ended up waiting tables in the middle
of the middle of nowhere, schlepping all the spaghetti
the unsuspecting could eat.

If we wanted beauty, open mic wasn't the place
to find it: the phthisic boy whose T-shirt read "Endure Pain"
or the two Tri Delts lip-synching the James Taylor songbook.
It felt good, another cheap beer sliding down, to know
we hadn't missed much never trying out for "My Fair Lady"
or mastering more than "Chopsticks."

That banjo player windmilling the same two chords
over and over, he might have been me,
blissfully superfluous, like Godzilla kicking hell out of Tokyo,
until he finished, almost dripping, a wound, agape,
annulled in stage light, a fierce dust falling on everything.

# Spoons

For a while afterwards he forgot to tumble off
bar stools, burn steaks and spit into salads. He forgot
what his ex-wife had said, forgot about the three cats,
all named Moe, his mother (dead) and his father
(also dead), forgot about his roommate, the crazy
tattooed florist. He forgot about salt and the '72 elections,
about Ronnie Lester's blown knee and Lute Olson, the week
he spent sleeping in the backseat of his broken-down
Ford Fairlane. He forgot he never took clarinet lessons
and didn't get to play Little League baseball,
forgot when he was a kid his father called him
Charlie Brown and didn't mean anything by it
he said. He forgot, happily, what his ex-wife hadn't said.
He forgot the correct spelling of catsup, the ten years
he wasted in the same dump of a restaurant,
how he'd never read Kant. He forgot to drink so much
he needed to cock one eye shut in the men's room
and gaze in a kind of epileptic splendor as each red
finger splintered itself into a nest of squalling hatchlings
he tried to use, never with much success, to knock
the big-toothed smile off the nearest big thing handy.
He forgot everything except what he begged us
to remind him over and over: how on an Iowa April night
he backpedaled blind-drunk off a balcony and did
a full-gainer onto the tarmac two stories below, dead
we worried, crippled we were sure, only to see him
rise, slapping away our hands and sobbing,
and pick up his six-pack of beer and brush himself off
with the bruised mien of a silent screen comic.
For a while afterwards he forgot to tumble off
bar stools and curse the help. He forgot
he carved only spoons and whittled a fork one day
instead. He forgot just how much he hated snow.

# Toxin

Some talk about a horse, a dead horse,
back up the road, by the cow pond,

and I go along, not to see the horse
exactly, but because there's this girl

I want to talk to, and on account of
it's Independence Day, also my birthday,

but for some reason I can't bring myself
to tell anyone. From a quarter mile off,

I say, That's no horse, it's a cow, but someone,
meaning this girl, says, It's a horse, and it is, tipped

on its side, legs stuck out stiff
like a knocked-over bed. And there's still

this girl, so I get close to the horse,
and it's beautiful, the coat spit-shiny

in the sun, the flies glinting madly
like ferocious race cars as they swim

over the soft parts, and I want, no,
I need to see this, and someone,

maybe the girl, calls, What's his
problem today, and I hunker closer

and I hear a voice, maybe it's the weed,
but I swear it's a voice, and it's telling me

part of a story, not words exactly,
but there's a voice, and when it's done,

I turn to everyone else, even the girl,
because I want to see them see this shining

in my face, but they're gone, long gone.

# The Flies

If God created flies, he perfected them,
their upside-down eyes and habit of being

everywhere first then departing last.
Like the uninvited guest who spills

wine on the rug, vomits in the bathroom
towels, and blacks out in the garage,

around his head a slick of oil, like evidence
at a crime scene or a shadow falling from

an angel's halo, its wings neither down
nor feathers but broken bottles and wire,

nightmares and iris petals collapsed
to the iridescent spoon of its back,

a tyrant's dream of a Catherine wheel.

## Poem for Women and for Men

*Do you want to know the disadvantages of having sex at my age?*
The old woman asked. *Flatulence, incontinence, and bruising.*
Sex will make a fool of us from the end to the beginning.
At age ten, in the stacks of the library
In the pages of a medical book of anatomical freaks
I saw a teenage girl. She was naked from the waist up,
Porcelain in a black and white photograph,
One arm raised in neither surrender nor salute, and in the armpit,
Small but fully formed, like an overturned doll-house tea cup,
A perfectly shaped, perfectly rounded miniature human breast!
And for a while afterwards, whenever a girl or woman would raise
    her arm
I'd do the quick eye dance for the third, the hidden,
Mysterious, rare, forbidden, the one part nobody ever mentions.

When desire begins to merge with imagination,
Under the blanket you pump the silky skin madly,
Probably no one told you how or told you why, with the full
    firm grip
Of a boy's fist from top to bottom and back up. The rush of fluid
Passing over exquisite nerves mixes with an irritating pain
As though you've fallen off your sled and careened, scraped and
    bleeding,
Wild with exhilaration, down a snowy hill. You don't yet know
About the rounded sensitive rim, the pacing, or the tenderness
You're supposed to show yourself as though you are another
    person
And that other person is supposed to be a girl!

Every child's organ with its own biography.

Like the twelve-year-old who unzipped my fly expertly with one
    hand, plucked my penis

From my underpants the way a man will arrange a book of matches
With one hand, fold a match forward to scratch it into flame,
Then slowly, idly, roughly, with the smallest part of her attention
While she chattered on the telephone, jerked me off.
I was also twelve, and frequently nudged her, stroke, stroke,
Until the white rope of marrow would geyser up
And over us, then with a Kleenex she wiped away the cum.

*She did what!* That's Gail, with her commentary.
And of her girlfriend she says: *At the café,*
*A really intimate conversation, the best of girl-talk, it had nothing*
*To do with men, by the way, then a man slides over to our table and,*
    *what!*
*She fluffs up her entire body like a hen in heat. She forgot I was even*
    *there!*


And somewhere between two cars locked bumpers, a clever angry
    woman
Saying calmly to an angry man, *You can   suck   my   cock.*

Anger, indignation, competition, confusion.
Sometimes beauty: In the Metro, from Bastille to L'Opera,
An aged couple, elegantly, shabbily dressed, their skin so opaque
    you could see
The jugulars flutter at their necks, and their mouths—dry leaves
Whispering into each other, kissing past station after station
With that certain passionate restraint. Chastened, we turned away.
Amazed, turned back to watch.

All night, asleep, a woman I'd just met held my penis sleeping in
    her hand.

Another night a woman and I were having this passionate
    conversation,
Half-intellect, half sexual tension, as though
We'd known each other for years and picked up where we'd left off,
And I could feel the night-crawler stirring in my lap
And then she said: *Isn't this great! I can have a good talk with a man*
*And not worry that at any moment he'll be trying to get into my pants!*

Separate creatures. Every woman with a rationale. Every man his
    plan,
And political ideas changing the ways we think.
No room for *Nice Ass* anymore, or *Let me carry that for you*,
No rude jokes, even with your wife, and in the company of the
    young
No shy and honest public airing
Of the struggle between men and women, and in educated
    company
Nobody even knows what to say anymore. *When did Romantic
    Love begin?*
Asks the professor before she tells us all, and the rooster wants to
    poke its head out
For a little look. Rue, regret, shame. She smelled so good
I was sure I could inhale her with a single breath.

*All women the same woman*: You write it in your notebook. Erase
    it, write:
*Separate creatures.* After that you write: *Rue. Regret. Shame.*

Do you know this? Of course, but I hope it doesn't strike you often
That somewhere a man, the husband of a friend, an uncle in his
    dotage,
Some invisible stranger who saw you on the street, your mind on
    groceries
A man stands over a toilet, eyes closed, hand moving, he grunts.
And further, further out and even weirder, a man is jerking off
To the girl you were thirty years ago
There he was peeping into your cabana. There you were
Changing out of your old bathing suit into your new pubescence
And in the foggy mirror the rosy aureoles
Of nipples rose to greet the cold,
And now the man can't get the picture to leave his head.

*You prick! You bastard!*
*You're all the same. All you do is follow it around.*

The elderly professor said: *I never chased women*
*When I was young. Who had the time? And wouldn't that mean*

233

*All women would become as objects? But the breasts—every year*
*They drop another inch. I still can't take my eyes off them.*

*Are they sensitive?* Gail shrugged. *Can I touch them?* She wouldn't
      let me.
We were looking for a place to put our blanket, and to please me
She scanned the women on the beach. This was Nice. She was
      pregnant,
Her breasts already swollen, so despite my protestations she kept
      them covered,
And with the artist's quick eyes located what she saw to be the
      most beautiful,
Most various congregations, spread our blanket out, and began:
This pair, that pair, the melons, the rockets, the wings of angels
      lying on their backs,
And at a distance two pretty teenage topless girls at volleyball.
*You see,* she said, as though it were perfectly obvious, *it's not the size,*
*It's the shape, the shapeliness. It's the proportion to the body.*
What does a man want? Are we all the same? And what to do
About the elderly woman who sat beside us at summer's ease,
And beside her, the granddaughter, both unmindful of my stare,
Both topless, serious as gamblers at their game of cards,
The cute little girl as yet unburdened by a man's inappropriate
      attention,
The woman's breasts unmindful after all these years were leathery
      and dark
As emptied Spanish wine skins, wrinkled as an old man's pair of
      slippers
What would I have done with them? *You're just a boy,* Gail said.
*All breasts are beautiful,* I countered.

*She'll do it with anyone, she doesn't care,*
My friend said. We walked up three flights of stairs and rapped at
      Bunny's door.
*Shh, my mother's sleeping.* One stuffed chair, one standing lamp,
One dull overhead. She didn't say another word, took off her
      blouse
And dungarees, her underpants, unhooked her bra, the breasts
      released,

Full and with the largest nipples I'd ever seen, sagged circles dark
    as plums.
She knelt, put her mouth on me till I got hard, pulled me down,
    pulled me into her
And we fucked—so this was what it was! My friend, on the stuffed
    chair,
Watching. At the door, *Kiss me,* Bunny said. At the dinner party,
    the guests
Were telling their shy stories, their earliest, most revealing, worst
    and best
And most bizarre sexual experiences. *How old were you?* a woman
    asked me.
*Thirteen.* Silence. *Jesus!* a woman said. Then: *Did you kiss her?*

And that remembered pick-up in a bar twenty years ago before
    disease
Gave its dire instructions, or your own wife who is the same
    woman each time
But somehow different. One night you talk about it, and she pulls it
Out of you. *You think we're all the same!*
Rue, regret. You write it in your notebook.

Then this: *Harder. Slower. I'm a grown-up woman now.*

In the medical book of anatomical freaks
The girl with a breast in her armpit
Looked to be about sixteen. I don't remember what she looked like
But she was smiling and I couldn't make out the meaning of the smile.
If still alive she's old by now. At best, she found a man who loved her,
A man with two hands and one mouth, but where
To put them, even after all these years, and in which order?

## Problem, Explained, Answered

\*

This mother blinks, then
that if

you will and perhaps you have heard of that
which is called synchronic

which is that which is best.

The poets rely on words as the urchin, the scuttled hull.

\*

There is no room
for you here
is some semblance of room for you.

I'd will an entire estate because I like your eyes
in which I'm a milky semblance of some man off
in somnabulus.

\*

There is never breezes in your poems,
are never breezes. No lush total
fissure for you're some man of mind.

Men of mind wander fro yet
never to stop.

There're hives around them but their eyes
betray the incessant wandering.

# Rustic II

Her word is falling
from the roadside

    the weak would ask *Why is it that you fall from me*

but I am not weak    just
overcome by heights


        new evidence puts me high up
        in some territory, some yellow

        territory, not exactly dusty,
        not exactly what I'd hoped

            her hair would do to the sun,
            filtering cliffs with its wavure


cliffs in her hair / from or of her hair

## Quietly from Lovell Street

Quietly

    Hannah

Quietly

    's last
    Words

Over

    The telephone

        *i.) Palms holding open*

        *ii.) Streetlight edged with winter*

The window now
Bricked-in where once

    The two
    Of them

Appeared

    Walking

The dazzling
Blue hue

    Across
    Lovell Street

Each morning

## Mozart's Requiem

They have lived a stone life, a star life, a rat life,
tears wiped out by the Siberian wind, packages wrapped
in despair,
moved from prison to prison, from age to age.

We used to bury our people, carve a cross, play Mozart's Requiem,
they started a new era of solitude
and loss,
their corpses our trees, our roads,

tones of blood evaporating in the air we breathe,
corpses lost in the tide of all times, high tide
on our empty beach, the grave

we don't deserve, the thoughts we never thought,
most of you don't even know why and for whom you are crying,
don't see their faces, don't hear their trumpets

when they happen to pass by your door.

# The Voice I Don't Have

1.
The voice I don't have is the voice I want,
yours,
broken in pieces, spread out on the floor, hot shower
along my spine,

your voice, star, trembling at the edge.

2.
And yours,
tall man with the afternoon light in your hair,
separating humans from gods,

one finger from the other . . .
voice that roars when the music stops,
the damp, the need to open the window,

your voice,
little dead mother     they nailed your coffin,
lashed the night,

they nailed and nailed until something went wrong,
sounds returned to their place
and merged into one word . . .

# Night

I love the night. In the morning,
my husband's mother loves him and bakes him
an apple pie. In the morning, he

wakes early and writes clever
poems to place on her doorstep. My time is the night.
Negative of his positive. The world

in which I am loved—because it is
not the world. But the world's moon, its reflection. My mother
only wanted to nap. I can see that

now, because I have become her.
It was not the nap. At three in the afternoon.
It was the solitude. It was

reprieve from daylight. She made a stab
at the tourist hot spots, the wholesome outings. By
afternoon she couldn't stand the homilies,

the group leg iron. She had to go
to bed!  I am just like her. My father's new girlfriend
hands me the tourist highlights

from the local paper—the boardwalk
art show and dolphin jumping—
and I hand it directly

to my husband. My father's new
girlfriend is a morning person. She doesn't have a
mean streak. After one hundred years of

terror, we flock to her,
cling to her daylight. She says the words
my mother said, calls my father

by his nickname, but it's weirdly substanceless,
like suddenly she's the night and my mother,
day. My mother had

dark hair and Ellen has light,
and so on. My mother had the courage of her convictions.
She did not do yoga. She did

not get massage. She liked a
rare steak and a glass of whiskey—but only one. All things
in moderation, even her lurid dying. She

said, We Ladies of the Old
South rise above it; she carried *The Way of All Flesh* in
her blue night bag for her last

trip to the hospital. She knew she was
out of air. She knew that nowhere on earth, in this life,
was there enough oxygen for her.

I wept for six months
about her life. About how there was no
element for her. She never

looked comfortable,
not in her childhood photos and portraits,
not in all the years I knew her. She

came to life a little in
the twilight. Her once-daily cigarette at sunset
on the beach. She loved the shore,

the margin, the entrance to
the wild, other, world. I wept because living
seemed agony to her, and love,

the worst. I kept saving things
to tell her. Most of the letters I wrote to her, I tore up
or put aside. I was saving stories

for that other place, our own
dead letter office, a place without shadow,
that paradise, the night.

# My Mother Turns Blue

My mother is turning blue. Her
fingernails are blue. She's going to leave
me alone on this earth, loyal

to her blue self and no
one giving a shit. I go in the dress store
where she always took me. I identify

myself as her daughter and they
don't care. Without my mother, I'm not
anything, and to top it off,

they don't ask me about her. Where
is she? Has she dropped off the face of the earth
since the last six-hundred dollar

suit? They stare at me
blankly, the young pretty blond one who is
evasive about the expensive

pants suit I want to buy—without
my mother I am street scum, hence can't
afford to buy a suit—who wears a huge

enamel cross on her perfect cute chest. Cute
enough to punch. And the made-up older one, the
one in drag, who lavished attention

all over me last summer, but when
I come in alone this time, without the dowager, hides
in the back room till I head for the door. I want to

brain both of them: My mother is blue!
How can they be so oblivious? What on earth is
their signal? Then, the fiddler

crabs at the beach, all fiddling away
with their oversized claws, hurling sand out of holes, or
simply sitting staring, at me: who am

I, and where is my blue mother? Born
yesterday, some of them, and the rest, last week, they
seem to remember my mother's and my

morning coffees thirty years ago, up the coast
in New Jersey. The poofy cream-filled donuts
from Ed's market, the *only* store

on the circle in Cape May Point, the sun
already getting hot at 9 AM. They remember it all and
are perched on their haunches

waiting to see if I do. And how will I
prove it? Final exam proctored by fiddler crabs. I pull my blue
book from my beach bag. And tell the whole

story. Of my blue mother. The story no one
gives a shit about—not the women at Levy's
certainly. Not the young surfer/drug dealers who

hang around our rented house on 81st Street.
No one in this town knows my mother grew up here,
that her father helped build this resort. The

effort the clerk at the souvenir
shop goes to to avoid *any kind* of friendliness, or
eye contact. The tourist freeze-out. The buggy

blank eyes of fiddler crabs which stick
straight up on little stalks from their heads,
the J.D. drug dealers, the willfully

apathetic grocery store clerks—are they trying
to remind me of our daily walk to the post office,
chagrined if there was no mail? Those were

the days of handwritten letters from home
in powder-blue envelopes. My mother liked to
        ride a rickety bike. She liked to smoke an occasional

                cigarette after dinner on the beach. But
that was years ago. It certainly wasn't enough
        to turn her blue. My blue mother.

                How she used to brood in winter.
Every day at noon an ancient guy in Bermuda
        shorts makes the journey from 81st Street

                to the composite-material bench
halfway up the slatted walkway to the beach.  He
        ogles the girls in bikinis as they file by.

                When I approach, he nods
like an iguana, his reflex capability somewhere below
        that of the fiddler crabs, the Levy's

                shop women. I'm going to read
him my final exam in my spiral
        book; I'm going to tell him the story

                of my mother who turned blue.

# High Romance and Everlastingness

I'd bust in, hardly conscious of him hardly consciously removing,
from the desk, his fee, and from his mouth—to meet my kiss—a strong cigar.
What a month of May we'd made inside that August day!

Knowing where I stood—between the radio and microwave—
I mamboed, mop in arms. Any metamorphosis was possible.
Didn't marriage mix romance with everlastingness?
    While winter breezes nabbed the leaves from peony trees
outside the pantry window,
I tango-spun toward spring.

Let him dash for buses that dashed off with him. Governor of the den,
I suspected life in love was self-sufficient like no other—if there *was* another.
I *knew* there was no other so magnanimous. A little summer sun, dovetailing
through Venetian blinds, could stripe with light the kitchen table,
letting me dissolve into the Yangtze Gorges I was drawing
on a small tomato box from the grocery store.

If he vanished in a book, sorted pencils, sat in shorts before the fan,
or cursed the Bears all fall from his La-Z Boy: betrayal. He was alien.
Staggering home from tennis in the spring, he'd meet his match: belting out
"Volare" from the bath I'd run for him. If I saw him scribbling at his desk
in his tiny script, I had to tap-dance in. He'd kick me out—but only when
I'd listen to his "Tristan," accompanied by compact disc.

Again, winter. Face to corner, hands on ears, eyelids clenched,
I hibernated, like my mother, never wondering if he wondered where I was,
while I, asleep, grew conscious I had born a snuggling cub.

Back by spring to Lincoln Center reveries, I wore white wings. I knew
I'd never bowed for any crowd but him, applauding in my dreams.
When he slipped beneath my skin, I wished to bleed for him alone.
Only on our double altar would I ever sacrifice my much too-private life.

That fall, as I edited my stand-up comic daydream, I spilled his tea,
mistaking for a china cup the hand I counted on for holding me.

Cruising on our summer honeymoon, we'd landed on the wrong
Aegean beach. We'd hardly slept—scared, dressed, on a stranger's roof—
waking to *our* island, transfiguring in glistening blue on blue . . .

Every time I pull my nightshirt overhead, he strums a tone poem
on my upraised arms. We jump onto the comforter as if into a skiff. He says,
*Love-slave, We're free all winter.* I say, *Let's clean house.* We know we know
as one all the photos in the hall: Tanzania; Zambia; the Congo . . .
In comparison, the Japanese weeping cherry tree—my study view,
busting fuchsia in the spring—has come to seem improbable.

Spying on him through a door-hinge, I contemplate unlikelihood:
What's to stop his intellect from merging with my flightiness? His dignity /
my delight? Our substances / spirits? Aren't our separate myths conjoined?
In winter, like my mother, I stuff cracks with towels, don't go out
except to scrounge for facts to heat "The Evening News." On that repast,
he's off to life and fantasy before returning home, escapee from a storm.


Mamma's gone, and we've grown older, feeling no less young.
From spring to spring, my sweaters bring the dresser drawers
their violets. His magazines have seen the house—

a villa, tilted on a rock. A painting propped upon an easel, stripped
of all the other pictures superimposed and underneath,
unveiling a transparency that limits the reality it translates into masterpiece.
Constructed out of resonance fortified by sympathy heightened by
the resonance, it's a life that looks like life, an edifice with window screens
shimmying in heat that hums when dragonflies come by to drop
some dragonfly-wing dust.

# Bozos, Bimbos, Scapegoats, Scum

He made us talk. Like the river—*Had it fallen in the night?*
Mornings, on the bridge, the District would turn out and make its call.
He walked by, and colors streamed behind him, a comet's tail
so vivid, no one saw it split the town—which never liked itself for long.
Even We remembered his off-moments: he'd fling himself
on *bimbo*-mercy: *It was Awesome; now I'm gone.*
Every lapse made him, to Them, an *alien bozo thug.*
They accused him—*liar scum*—of crooked river-soundings. Once,
that current cleared a girl who'd been branded "Satan's Bride." A lover
chucked by Puritans to rapids any witch would ride, she'd sunk.
The new U.S. Red Guard, out to ransack *stinking enemies,*
began to drag the waterway. A Counselor and a Big Blonde surfaced,
dumping dredged-up sludge upon the Commons.

Shrieking, *"Smear"* and *"Clean-up,"* We and They stampeded.
Obscenities seeped through trench coats covering, like thugs', our heads.
The Law was on the lam. Nakedly gyrating, the river stripped off spray,
arousing the susceptible: *Grab the real bare-asses of imagined foes . . .*
Chimes divided Catholics, Jews, Bone-Agains—most unfaithful,
more irreverent, all infected by the fossils slung from slime riled by roar.
*Sleazebag* thrust cuffed hands to us: *I never trampled, forced, extorted . . .*
*Touch my un-malicious wrists; trust me; I need air.* Rivals nailed his sores,
grabbed his larynx, stabbed his potency. Any hurt was just
if it subverted his subversion of their pure authority. *Their* side—
electrified loose iron—was righteous, like the Media.
The Blonde advised the *slut: One smart dress will take you far . . .*
The Counselor met her *ho* protests: *Let lips that can't say no confess—*
*or get two decades in the joint for Femaleness.* Her taunted stalker flesh,
revving pulses, stained the meat-men's aprons muscle-rust and cream-desire.
Uncorking his'n her hard drives, basting with one word, SEX,
568 times—to turn those chaos taste-buds on, the Counselor led the roast
of *Demon Flesh on Rule of Law.* Soon, we'd eat our own.
Some turned spits; some sat transfixed. Some among *the Public*—
bucking stallion led to water—would not drink the venom-stink.
*We'd* outshine the fire! With snapping backs and neon faces,
we sang: *Israelis! Palestinians! They're used to having pins stuck into them.*

In the abject reveries of Freshmen Congressmen, Lust and Hustle—
grossly swollen, blooming ice-pick wounds—wave white flags:
*We've seen Paree; now get us home to prove our common bonds.*
*We'll fix the general loss of grip by doing it with everyone.*
From the true home, loneliness, a lone soul, ideal-struck,
had waded toward Town Meetings. But each of us thought the other
thought himself better—didn't he?—and better off—he didn't.
We'd need representatives:
*Father Scapegoat Husband Liar Devil Lover Martyr Son.*

Rooting into city-shards—smoldering ochre in a witch-puce riverbed—
we discover mirrored scraps. On charred docks, black saints catch whiffs
of brimstone and lift their moonshine cups to the whipped of recent history.
Drifting down, the spirits toast: *Assimilate yourself. Call your upsets*
*"evil flukes"—they'll repossess you.*

At sunset, colors bleed:
*touch us, trust us . . . Or go on—*
*drown in blues that drown in blues.*
*Suck up gold and roses.*
*Revel in citrines, garnets, amethysts, and emeralds: every drop*
*you wring from anyone.*

# Fair Seas, A Back-up Breeze

Growing up, the explorers told their logbooks: *Fill!*
Hockey pucks went in. Catamarans. Browning; Kipling; Dickens . . .
countless navigation aids. Sweet, clean, shaving dreams. And prophesies
of ocean crossings, flying home above calm sea, fulfilled as well-fed gannets.
  These darling, cocky boys needed school chums, like me,
cheering them past unacknowledged, rocking clouds of doubt.

Young Virgil would have fit right in—standing out—with them.
To hear them think, these port-side skippers could adapt to anything.
  Swaying heel to heel in suspenseful library calm, they tuned
their compasses and souls to all the coasts they'd opened in their hopes.
  Panting brilliantly, they skidded through the stacks—why study
evolution's pitfalls? It had mothered *them*, their expansive aspirations.

Tied, by natural habit, to those resembling them in ascendance,
manhood, origin, they dipped into Euripides, Shakespeare, Darwin, Freud—
Why dwell on flaws? Death was just an antique borrowers' card.
Why check out the flops, like Walter Raleigh?—though a glance suggested
he'd been *one of them*—no traitor, as he'd seemed. Before his execution,
he, too, had tried, in upper dark, to plumb the novel, long-sought stars.

At their launching, linen lengths scooted flag-like up their masts,
joining gulls they matched. I called, *Take me? Or stay? I live for your tall tales!*
*Tell me the Aleutian goose is not a threatened species! Tell me time's not fatal!*
  Soothed, from the pier, by the dazzling, opaque bay, I clutched
*Selected Shelley*; in my hands, it overflowed with longing. I called,
*Fair seas! A back-up breeze! Leave your lives to find them! Don't drown trying!*

The mariners made *terra incognita*, sunlight split on wakes they rode.
Lulled by wave-pit snow, they aged. Jittery, they pulled out maps:
*The Voyage of the Beagle; The Future of an Illusion; The Renaissance* . . .
  They pitched in squalls. Stalled. Radio out, sextants shot, they got old.
Had they had it? *BOOM!* They got it: *We can Move this Odyssey!*
*With tide-shifts—winds we can't predict—extra engines—bulletins* . . .

Oh Captains, keep tapping back your gorgeous SOS: a signal phrased
exquisitely from your helplessness; a link between land's end and oceans' meeting
at land-links; music's edge—in victory's 'V'—around the sounded undertows
to unbounded, bounding mains; a communiqué, two way, across the latitudes.
    Crane or kite can glide beyond Beyond, but visionary language, gliding
past a kite or crane with age-old give and take, may unlock nature's dominance.

    Only tell us, my Tall Ship, has your wooden figurehead—
the girl with breasts and fins and wings—
pointed out the planet's rim, always racing closer?
    Tell us, if you glimpsed it, how you turned about and tacked back through
typhoons and starving octopi to constellation-canopies; dolphins who mistook you
for their own; and healthy schools of striped and spotted dwellers in the depths.

And how, climbing water walls along untried Great Circle Routes,
you caught new travelers' "MAYDAYS!"—just before they felt your tug,
and tugged back on the satin line of fragile buoys tying them
to all of the endangered—the living; dying; thriving; you.
    Then tell about your guillemots, diving into liquid space,
and how your petrels still burst out.

## Of Stars and Water and Instructions
## for Observing Both

Sometimes it's best to understand nothing,
unless you can see how, in the future, it's all going
to come crashing into the water—the gory end
of things, the blood and the tall, cool glasses
lined up around the pool's lip, where the body floats,

bobs, really, with the uncontrolled movement
of lack. Lack of breath. Lack of volition. If floating
like that is the only tragedy you ever encounter,
it's enough. You shouldn't have to fear anything
else, but doesn't living interfere with that ambition?

Every day new calamities to consider, every
day new messes made in the haphazard
way of thoughtless grace—you make me,
for instance, see that my entire orbit
has been around the wrong planet,

that my calculations were off from the beginning.
I'm no astronomer—the stars guide me
by existence, not position,
since charts and visions by their natures
are contradictory. I'm a master at contradiction:

witness the lonely and satisfied heart I carry
behind my breast, the topsy-turvy signals
battling it out in my skull—none of this
would have happened if not for appetite—
how long since I stood inside myself and felt

my skin fit? All the hungers rising up—
like a telescope pointed at the right star, the one
where an event will occur that shakes up
the community of science, the star-gazers,
the kids necking in a car, even the raccoon

crossing the road and disappearing
into the denseness of the forest—all the hungers
for knowledge or passion or change, or simpler
things, a glass of orange juice
and a piece of buttered toast—all of this

reminds me of dislocation. All of this reminds me
how many blank pages are in the book.
There's a different remedy for every ill,
but you can also use the same one every time:
know yourself. Which symptoms will respond

to touch. Which you can ignore and hope
will go away. But there's still the corpse
in the pool, the floating specter of your life
that has to be fished out. Face what's next:
Grab the net. Make all the necessary calls.

# Knowing

Unless there's something else to do,
I'll take a card. Another. Oops.
That's the trouble with not knowing,
with the nature of a game

or sorcery: you don't know
until *after* you needed to.
Which sense is most important
to you? I can see that

it's sight, the grand elision
of all that's left unseen. Today
I saw everything on sale.
Tomorrow I'll see if I'm still

in the game, in the pink,
in the aftermath of upheavals
that make Chernobyl and
Mount St. Helens synonymous

with my life: I'm not in prison,
but some of what I'm thinking
ought to put me there.
I'm holding on to sight, though,

still ranking it right up there
with the feeling of a favorite quilt
on a cold evening, and the fire's
gone out, cool draft from the flue

entering the room like a cloud
that's lost its way. Something
in the nature of heat tempts
me toward all the wrong things:

the wrong men, the wrong clothes,
an incorrect attitude toward
history and the number eight,
which winds infinity around me.

Tonight the orphans and barn swallows
conflate into one song:
How will I know when to leave?
I couldn't tell you what it is,

but there's some kind of testament there.
I know it's wrong to go
out of my way to criticize myself—
I'm doing what I have to do

and loving it. I'm doing what every
stupid alley cat takes for granted—
get some when you can, yowl
about it if you must.

## Poetry

Miss Moore called it "fiddle," and although I might use
"occasionally irrelevant churning, like an outdated
washing machine," essentially, I agree with her.

Moon shadows on snow, Orion chasing the Pleiades.
Sweet work indeed, whether or not I write about it.
But if I were to apply a mathematical precision

to this sprawling constellation, I would fold neat piles
of words, line them up on a bed.  Make random outfits.
A simple collection of pink:  Pepto-Bismol sidles up to cheek.

Or a question of four-letter words: moon fart sing when?
They'd wait there all day, unable to complain when the cat
sits gaudily on them, grooming her private particulars.

Then when long-sleeved "love" begins to misbehave,
mixing in with the duck boots when it should stick
to cotton underwear, I'll shove it in a bottom drawer,

dance to some Etta James, get drunk on wine.
Sweat through my bra.  Wallow in my own blessed
irrelevance, in my own sweat, that other form of crying.

# When I Don't Know What to Write
# I Write Haiku

Hammer-bangs outside my window. Someone's building
    something.
One way to look at it: there's scaffolding around my heart,
but everyone's on lunch break.
The light comes into the window slowly. It's not yet on my face.

*There goes my good mood:*
*a grape. Sweetness swallowed, then*
*nothing on the tongue.*

So much churning for so few syllables, when really,
the grief I'm trying to nail down
lives in the white space. There's a branch outside my window.
It's waving to me with its little stick fingers. Or maybe it's
    scratching the sky.
Could the sky have an itch?
Q: What's brown and sticky?
A: A stick.
I think that one's funny.

*Why these tiny lines?*
*Invisible roads. In this*
*poem, near my eyes.*

So you could say it's kind of a control vs. effluence thing, a
    disrupting
language thing, what seems to be an adjective
has really more to do with a noun. It's sticky.
Whatever. I'm going to take a nap.
My sister used to say, I don't want to kill myself; I just want
to take enough pills to fall asleep for a couple weeks.
I can see the appeal.
The hammering has stopped.
Nothing.
Suddenly, I feel like I'm praying.

*The heart doesn't stop;*
*it just holds itself, waiting*
*for the next big spin.*

I know the tiny lines have something to do with control,
I know there's comfort in the vastness
of white space.
I think *I don't have to fill that if I don't want to.*
Q: Is there a way to exist between
the words and the white?
In that betweenness
of time, when you know the match is lit,
but it hasn't yet started to burn?
A: I have one last period, so before
I use it, I would like to say
I don't know, I don't know,
I don't know.

# A Dream in Four Parts

### 1.

You call me from a payphone in Queens.
I can see the boarded-up shops behind you,
a newspaper blows by your feet.
You've been dead for nine years.
I ask, *Why aren't you in heaven?*
*Don't worry, sweetie,* you say.
*It shouldn't be that much longer.*

### 2.

I am drunk in a ditch.
I am burning from the inside out
and breathing
as little oxygen as possible.

### 3.

This time, you're alive.
You ask me who this woman is that Dad married.
I'm too used to you being gone
to have any sympathy,
so I just say, *You know, when you talk,*
*dead leaves come out of your mouth.*

### 4.

You use my father to demonstrate:
*This is how you please a man.*
You lift your head from his stomach,
and your brown-tipped breasts graze your arm.
*Who did you end up marrying?* you ask.

# Twelve Images that Entered Christ's Head as He Stood Crucified

A gauzy light shimmers in the distance, a veil, a scarf.

Crows perch on a wire, a sentence missing *crow* as word.

Lead-bellied clouds scuttle across the sky, beggars or exiles?

A crab picks up a candle, holds it against its other claw, says *pain*.

The same horse has been neighing in the distance, bitter hour
in its mouth.

A fly lands on his left hand, in its eye a thousand crucifixions.

Blasphemy reddens the earth, pales the grass, rains heavenward.

Only a shadow, slanted against the cracked earth, knows the
difference between night and day.

Behind closed eyelids, he sees the vast horizon, lines fracturing,
shaping into a yellowing whirlpool.

Who is this woman with the covered face? Sand flying into her eyes,
her feet rooting into the soft earth.

A wood dove pecks out the red sinew from his side wound, tugs
at it in jerky motions, fluttering toward its half-finished nest.

Light fades into a scarf, a radiant river, minnows slivering
through.

# Scatological Christ

After reading a book called *Merde*, written
by a mechanic or engineer who has spent
the last 30 years studying feces, I can't help
but think of all the times I've heard news
of presidents and popes on NPR and thought
of all the words for shit in Spanish, the way
I always heard my father say it, slurred,
a bit bilious between the teeth, like acid
returning into the mouth after a spaghetti
dinner: *mierda, crapula*, or my favorite
*retama de guayacol*, which to this day I know
not what it means or where it comes from,
but when my father called someone that,
I knew the conversation was over. Reserved
for the times Fidel's name came up, or his
brother Raul. And I ponder why such words
exist. Why we use them at all. What would
we be without them. Our lives so much
emptier without hearing the old man next
door curse his life, the uselessness of his years.
Or the countless jokes Cubans have for shit.
Or someone who ate it. There should be
a prayer for dung. A saint too like Emygdius,
saint of earthquakes, or Cabrini, saint for
immigrants, or Marculf, saint of skin diseases.
A saint of bowel movements, Saint Rumbliose.
Something like that. Or a suave Cuban-type
Christ, who once risen from the dead, might
say: *Esto sigue siendo trememda mierda!* That's what
I need—a Christ who pinches shut his nose
at all the foulmouths and blasphemers like me.

# Christ of Tourette's Syndrome

*Have you come here for forgiveness?*
*Have you come here to raise the dead?*
*Have you come here to play Jesus*
*to the lepers in your head?*
                              *—U2*


*We called him El Jeferson, because he pronounced*
*his name in Spanish: "Me llamo el Jeferson Fernandez."*

*We beat him up during the basketball games in gym,*
*dragged him over the cement until his knees bled.*

*His eyes rolled into the back of his head and frothy*
*saliva webbed the corners of his mouth, then he'd start*

*to mouth all these curses in Spanish: "Putos! Jotos!*
*Pendejos! Putosjotospendejos! Putosjotospendejos!"*

*He'd say it over and over until we were all bent over*
*holding our sides trying not to choke on our own*

*laughter. We kicked him, spat on his hair, kicked*
*up dirt into his mouth. Then when the teachers*

*ran toward us, we took off over the fence. How many*
*truancies didn't we already have anyway? We only*

*came to school to kick Jeferson Fernandez's ass.*
*"Tijuanero!" we shouted back at him. "Wetback!"*

*Some said the trouble with Jeferson started at birth*
*when his mother dropped him on his head, and we*

*loved to watch him twitch, and then start shouting:*
*"Hijos de puta! Hijos de puta! Putosjotospendejos!"*

*Tantric quality of Spanish words still aglow fire-red.*

# Exit Jesus

How could I not lose my way in the cold penumbra, crow
    wing vastness of those long ago Madrid churches, a couple
    of basilicas my mother, *la devota*, took me to, then later
the two nuns in the family when they visited from Seville

one summer? I sat there on the hard pews, almost twelve,
    confused by ritual, how the knots and swirls on so much wood
    spoke to me between all the sitting, kneeling, standing . . .
The women dressed black, knitting veils over their eyes,

wrinkled faces, rosaries dangling from their thin fingers.
    Then the lining up for the holy communion, the priest,
    pasty-faced, white hands like scaled gutted fish, fingers worm-
like in the basket, the pinched host cracked in his fingers,

and each time he slipped one on my tongue I walked back
    chewing openly, thinking of the fish in a bowl, rabbit ears,
    my mother elbowing me because she thought I was being
disrespectful—and I'd chew and look up at those huge ceilings,

the lights breaking through the stained glass windows, casting
    green and gold hues over everything, and I'd feel dizzy, my stomach
    fooled once again, rumbling, and as hard as I tried to concentrate
on the priest's litany and piety (Latin gibberish), I couldn't stay

still, and then a new cycle of kneeling, praying, standing . . .
    too much for one who'd never learn the meaning of what came
    naturally to most—I knew then my days in the church would be few,
and my hands sweated, and I tried to imagine a man named Jesus

in all of this: the wood pews, golden candelabras, chalice, ceilings,
    the saints all lined up, waiting, wax glossed over their eyes. Yes,
    I wanted to stand and shout, the Host has left the building, the Father,
the Son, the Holy Spirit—into this unforgiving brightness waiting

for all of us, my mother, me, the batty old ladies to enter the world.

# The Pines

*a Millay Colony journal*

A manse, the word for it,
a grand private mansion,
and yet it seems to me
the last of civilization,
where it is just pinned to the trees.

A white housefront,
a right angle
against feathery dark.  Of course,

you can't escape its beauty.
It slashes through
like the best knife.

\*

I am afraid for that shack
by the side of the road.
People poor in that way, exposed
to winter.  Snow outside
each time they'd look.

But this summer night,
moths flatten against the glass
like still-hungry ghosts.
A gloating moon marbles the trees,
makes a graveyard of day.

\*

I wake to such clear definition,
sun scattered along the ground.
I feel the press of the mountains.

All day a scent of crushed berries,
so few words spoken,
I'll remember each one.

\*

For hours I stare out of myself
at those trees, not
as a painter does, not to remember,
only to get past them.

\*

Like patterned silk,
the mower's circles in the grass.
I walk to the ruined pool,
sprays of insects at its surface,
stone cherubs nodding.

Then the outdoor bar, jagged wood,
curtained by ferns.
I imagine a shimmer of party guests.
Lupine in the raised
flower beds and columbine,
wheel moving within wheel.
All of us waiting for dark,
for the blur of anything
we can still make out.

\*

Wind searches the low branches,
vibrato of desire.

Think of them,
whole afternoons, making love,

one threaded into the other,
wild shadows sweeping over them.
The wolf comes out
in your face then,
there's such desperation.
Oh, that poor excuse, that human body.

\*

I follow a gravel path
until moss softens my footsteps.
Approach at last
the cul-de-sac at the gravesites.
A breeze or an insect
just lifts the hair from my forehead.

Then what a scrambling
and clutching of branches,
while I remark to myself
the steady spires of trillium.

Like opera:  billowing voices,
wind leavening the trees, storm cloud
like an arm raised behind them.

\*

The thunder god, the axe.
When the tornado came
it bit away the top third of the trees
in their long watch by the drive.
People say a stray dog got in then
and ran for the cellar.

\*

Inside the barn, thin sunlight
criss-crosses a weft of spider web.
Damp comes in, the moist outdoors
on each breath I take.

*

This is what a story does, lay crumbs
along a path.

       In the thickest part
of the pines, all that remains
is a soft red fundament of needles
where nothing grows.

# Devi

A woman who's a cuckold,
you understand, becomes
a kind of goddess.  She could reach
for the round sun over a shoulder.
Sometimes it's so cluttered
anywhere she looks, the sky
is the only clear space.  Not horns,
her friends mount on her forehead
a crown of astonishment
and understanding.  And she
is welcomed someplace part coffee bar,
part beauty shop, praised for
her willingness to know a man's body,
without knowing anything.

An hour before she was moaning
into her cell phone, Sugar, sugar,
where are you? Those same friends
have since become an army of Amazons
in their ceremonial and practical use,
and she, a deity of revenge.
All the weapons are on her side,
dagger, bow, noose and goad.
The power of will, the prod to action.
Suchness, thatness, cosmic night.
And even so, she'll go back to him,
with sixteen arms and a gold sari.

# Ghost Wife

Out from the trees, the skinny
fox and the vixen, starved
for they scarcely knew what.

The river moved in its ring
of stubborn flowers,
a broken mirror filled with light.

I remember butterfly wings
rubbed to a colored powder.
The corn cut in rows like crosses.

Yesterday, I was living and today,
here, hovering over things.

Then your face blundered
through the long,
blond strands of spider web.

How have you found me?
How have you come back
through all the black rooms to me?

# The Fork in the Moment

Sometimes a sentence has to go forth
into the world like an eldest child
and be the first one, the only kid in the class
who knows all about sex,
and has to live with the secret knowledge,
knowledge like the first fizz out of the soda bottle.

A car horn was honking and honking
in the woods by the construction site,
maybe somebody calling for help,
its rhythm the only key to its meaning.
It was steady for a while, purposeful,
then let silence and twilight wash over it
for a few minutes, then resumed,
then stopped. I didn't go down there;
I didn't call the police. There was nothing
about it in the paper all week.

Remember Toby Tyler,
the boy who ran off with the circus?
And Huck with his slingshot,
zinging crabapples at cars?
We hid out in the woods
on the near side of adolescence,
barefoot, starting fires with a stick,
never going home.
We had a pact to live outside
the adult world forever,
and we broke it.
I climbed the chain link to get in,

dropping down hard
so that I felt my feet in my jaws.
We lost each other. Nothing was left
of the trees but stumps like gravestones:
Huck Finn, Toby Tyler, and me.

# Sorry

I'm to press the pad of my thumb
against the trout's upper jaw,
its teeth surprisingly sharp,
more like berry cane than teeth,
its eyes already beginning to look back
from the afterlife. It's limbless,
like a whole soul in my hands,
and slimy, so I clamp it
with my knees to get a better grip,
and use both thumbs
to force back the jaw until the spine
breaks slowly, like a green stick,
and the jaws half close
as if by failing memory.
Then later in the sink we slit
open the belly, strip out the guts,
see if it's male or female,
see what it's eaten. If it's female
Dad clicks *sorry* with his tongue.

# What the Grownups are Saying

Don't you want to hear
what the grownups are saying?
Let's eavesdrop from the balcony.
Those parties had currents,
an undertow of scent,
low-throttled approvals of male cars
idling through a three hour dinner
and come-what-may, more drinks later
and the bird-laugher pitched slightly high.
Mrs. M always played with the candles.
She'd snap off the weak stalagmites
and feed them back into the fire.
When the wives got drunk
they spilled secrets,
retelling the stories and adding
a few details no one knew,
then getting milked for the rest.
How Mrs. C stole Mr. M's clothes
skinny-dipping in '58,
and Mr. M walked into town
with a maple twig looking for a phone.
The two deer killed with one shot.
The talking ran like a brook through the house
then out into the icy lake of knowledge,
beyond the known words to where the water
began to smell like the sea,
and the first feathers of the undertow
began their inventive caressing.
Tonight we've found a box of Tampax
in Mom's bathroom, and just before dessert
we'll shoot all forty white mice with tails
over the railing into the perfumed clouds below.

I'm not hurting them, her and him.
I'm just keeping them locked
in these pronouns for a while
so I can study them,

almost-closing the door on them
but not quite. They're washing up,
the guests gone home,
and cannot hear that outside
in the background of the world
the voice of the party continues,
its words ascending the stairs
into the child's ear ad infinitum.

# The Built-In Accident

*A Marriage of Heaven and Earth*

Every time you think you're done, you're not—the moment
you choose to go back to. It's the meaning of romance,
    beforehand. Memory

thaws. Tiny flames out of cans.
Daybreak from the bottom of the pit. Surfacing fish in strict
    winter. Sly

gamekillers, you are guided by the Supper Star. Carried off,
    twirling.
(You must be very vigilant, or you will be taken away.)

The dog wouldn't budge from your heels for days. You have to
    understand
how humbling that was.

Fetal circumstance, mute place, triangulation. The contract of
    incest. Back then,
people marry people they don't love.

Conscience, I suppose, needs thinning. Has imagined
much: Land-owner, pig, born-again—a kind of hanging.

A kind of task, I call it *morning*.

# Heartbreakingly Small When You Sleep

exactly like epilepsy, arrhythmia

plus wanting alcohol. Snoring,
like dying.

As much as I would like you to, you won't
like a memory that has no possibility, or,

is startled.

I will take the sleep, exactly like you are. So then,
also

everybody wanted to talk about it, which is
a way of leaving me out. No better than

feeling sorry for, or finally meaning, or
to keep believing in myself as we will never

never stop talking about it. Or, for that matter,
it's my way of leaving anyone. Trick them,

temporarily, into thinking
my heart broken. Because they're so skinny and drunk.

And bored by my straight-forwardness. And then
the memory temporarily returns—

of two animals chasing each other in the city,
and we have no idea what kind of animals they are—

oh, this isn't fair. For that matter, you're so beautiful.

# Being a Great Believer in Cooling

There's a direction inside the mind
where I don't care to go too far        or into the heat

too far  of Arizona in August. They're both too much.
Cobalt blue lightened

it's so bright. And so hot you can't imagine.
Heating is disgusting. But the mind

isn't completely bad—imagination's orderly zeroes for heat
        counting to ten to bear it

as my mother counted to three and at three
punished me. Cobalt blue on the tiles of roofs

the color of parking lot lights on palm trees

and how the blue is solved by heat. There's something

inexplicably familiar about how
it disappears to the brightness—and who am I

with my mixed up feelings, like your 'want'

looking exactly like 'won't',
your lonely like lovely. Well,

that was exactly what happened: Blue,
lots and lots of it—and then sunshine.

## Signs

Such soft arms from the capped sleeves of my mother's
Christmas dress! She's sitting beside my father
back before he was my father. They're young, they're smiling,
the curtains are ruffly. The flashbulb
flashes back from a mirror propped against the wall.

I know how to walk into a kitchen
and scan it for signs of struggle:
Alphabetical soup cans, a matchbook
wrung to a toothpick, strawberry incense
over cigarette smoke and the phone cord
under the bathroom door.

I know what to do, how to twist a steak knife
from her fist. Bag in one hand, the other on her shoulder,
I know how to lead her past policemen, belt her to the car seat,
light the cigarette hanging from her lip.
I know how to wait in waiting rooms.
I know how to sign the forms.

Still, they're smiling. The curtains are white.
Christmas stockings hang from the mantle. Her legs
cross at the ankles. She holds one hand on his thigh
and the other in a fist. She sits on it.
I know it.
I know how hard.

# Pick It up Again

The end of an insistent autumn. Each tree
the obvious culprit of its yellow litterings.
The girl cutting two blonde braids off her bound head:
careful, careful to let each hank drop
directly into her dresser drawer.
Then the mother out of nowhere, and the girl
with less hair, confused by the trouble
given all the care she took to keep the floor clean.

How can winter mean anything
but desolation? Branches bony as the girl's hand
right where the father dropped it. The fact
of that hand and the father
feet ahead, composing a love poem for his next wife
while the girl waits, rooted in her red boots.
What was conversation is silent: the leaves fall
as if all at once, in bruise-colored clots and rings.

# Halcion

My mother is a text
in tiny script. Picture
a postcard: there's her body
tossed on the wide bed.

Inertia calls to me
in the slurred words
familiar as flat pillows
no washing can lift.

I go to the coast to read
the beach. Red shells
and gray gulls
litter the wet sand.

I go back to her mattress,
try touching her shoulder.
One orange fish
floats at the top of its tank.

I have my long-handled net.
I wave it. I wait.
Out the window, a raccoon
climbs the pine tree:

crows go wild with calls,
louder as he nears their babies.
It's Spring. Everything gets quiet.
I can hear the birds are breathing.

JOE WENDEROTH

# Defending a City Lost in Flames

You and I learn to read innocence
into every part of the room.
The chair, the little shoes on the wall,
the dirty white door.
What we could never bear to know
is offered to us continually:
the whole city lost in flames.
To say anything at all is to imagine
we are making a rush into the thick of it.

# Against Christian Love

Let the animal resume
abolition of its journey;

let the local certainties
of its brief good time
revolve as they will
in even surer fire,
obscured.

Let the day-long kissing of pain
bring no good standing
no real names.

Let the weak flame
I've been built up
out of
break its promise,
this very moment.

# In America

What is it that is making you famous?
Is it that you are the one
who knows where the body is?
Or is it that you know the body
will never be found?

## A Hundred Efforts Have Been Made

For the holiday party I make
myself a starfish costume
of glitter and gray latex.

You say all the girls
will be in the hospital after this one,

undone by chicken bones or petite seizures.

I say no, no one is trying that hard to have fun.

Sitting is difficult
but I can perform mini-pinwheels
with my body or sometimes just my eyes,

while the in-crowd debates the aesthetics of space needles.

Disguised as a serial killer, you wear leather
with bent tendons and a winning smile.

And we make a charming couple and people
are jealous and offer to take our picture

and then we step into a song by Elvis
and we go to hell all over again.

I drink and think:
the older I get the less ways there are
to hurt myself and still learn something.

I find you in the kitchen
Surrounded by olives and tiny forks

Oh, I love forks and you, the joyful conveyers of whatnot,
    needed.
Something I have kissed and licked for years.

At last, a normal vanishing,
my one and only trick.

# The Real Estate Agent Finds a Way

He has always tried
to use the little words
to explain what he means:
airy, easement, morning light.

See, dogs are no good—
they smell of the earth
and cannot be compressed
into a portrait of ownership.

But a cat
that will stay still
is an asset.

Twice divorced, he thinks
there is nothing like a vacant house
to swab religion into clean towels,
into the question of throw pillows.

Weeks of finessing,
resisting the urge
to fuck in the beds
of strangers. Anyone

can feel a custodial crime
and run, despite the fireplace.

They will check the deed
for artistry or imaginary punctuation,
they will flush the plumbing

until he is
ashamed to be human.

A house can never be a mystery.
He lives in two stories,
halfway between a ghost and a planet.

# If You Steal It, Is It Mine?

Cadillacs, says Rachel, aren't just for seniors anymore.
Elvis had a long black car.

If I lift up my shirt
on a good day, people will pay
attention. Don't worry about the sky.

The sky always looks like a reliable witness.
A witness replies that Rachel was never
as far from inspiration as she thought.

God does not speak through Rachel
and she's got no psychic powers
unless someone else
is watching.

Like that night last summer,
when the piano bar went up in flames.
Everybody cheered while I fell in love
with her dumb magic.

Her eyes are nothing but vision.
Hands. I say hands make the best disguises
and usually outwear brains.

Don't you like car games? Here is our impression of a car game.

Discuss how birds and bombs can bring us together.
Name 17 anonymous blue-green stars.
Tell us the best uses for gangplanks in heaven.

# What Majesty

Something evil
has never stopped arriving
in this office.

She experiments with paperclips and pills.
Taps out the alphabet backwards
to indicate the rate of exchange
on animated swords, the sound
of a dragon lady, weeping.

Tonight there must be people
from Japan to Minneapolis,
scattershot with ambition,
getting solid jobs,
their wives nodding,
good for them. Good for them,
getting and not giving,
ripening to the digital touch of god.

What if all she ever wanted
were luminous breasts and a dog at her feet
who sleeps through bad weather and eats well?

In arcadian dreams
all the coins are magic
and the blackbirds speak
English far better than here
in the boardroom where salesmen
dribble tips and smell,
signing on to whatever's budging
in vast American warehouses,

to raise it, sell it, buy it, kill it.

Oh, these action verbs
are too opaque and time is wasting

when she could be flat on her back
strewn with musky bughouse flowers
attempting to manufacture something

mythic out of elevators and velvet.

A softness, a gray rising and falling
so that she might have a good story
to tell when the job is over.

She is an itch coming on strong and the time is now,
for a love no longer mystified and hissing at the crowds.

## Back to Normal

Angel knows
she has a soul
a gypsy lover told her
he felt it fumbling
to unbutton unsnap
her she thought
it was leaves and twigs
beneath the blanket
he spread in the back
of his pick-up truck
he said her breasts
were pomegranates years
ago it was love now
Angel fucks
her new boyfriend says
she needs a conscience needs
to get more active
she signs a petition
for peace her mom
says he just wants
a piece the man on TV
says it's time
to get back to normal
Angel wants to go
to Food Lion to touch
a pomegranate wants
to believe her soul
is more than leaves
twigs beneath a blanket
in the bed
of a rusted Chevy
under a moonless
night but something
is missing

# Friday Before the Rain

My father's funeral lasts forever.
First the wicker chairs on the manicured lawn
turn black, legs crumble. Then the grass gives up.
We stand and rock from foot to foot, fold hands.
Look at the sky, my mother says. I look at her mouth.
When the rain begins, we rush for umbrellas, cars.
Except my father. He pouts. Where's my body?
Why are my shoes filled with ash?

When it stops, I am sixteen, sneaking into the house drunk.
Try not to breathe, talk too much. My shirt's stained
with Norman's garage-brewed vino. I've lost my shoes.
My mother and father are watching the news, the weather.
I stand there, try not to sway.
My feet grow roots. My father has no face

as he lifts me, carries me to the car.
We've spent the evening at the Aceto's.
The adults drink downstairs while I play upstairs
and listen to the music of their laughter rise
like smoke that eventually puts me to sleep.
It's like a miracle to me the way I close my eyes
in one place and then wake in another,
at home in my own bed. Maybe I stir
just a little as my father sets me in the car.
But sleep is what I want, this dream.

It's not a dream my father tells me. No, I tell
myself that death is like that car ride.
But this is all too easy. I'm afraid
that nothing is how I imagine it.
Drunk on wine aged for days, puke on the floor
by my bed, my mother hating my father
for dying, my father wishing he could open
his mouth to let it fill with rain. But he doesn't have
a mouth. And the rain hasn't started yet.

# In the 20th Town of Ghosts

*What does it matter what reality is outside myself?*
*—Baudelaire*

Not even I am here.
The sun sweetens my pot of misery.

Every step I take leaves tiny graves.

The animals I recognize from dreams.

Standing in the back-lit doorframe
pulling a silk robe across your cheek, you explain

how the shed in the yard was built in anger.
I hear the arguments of plank and nail.

As I open the one door, my life begins.

# CONTRIBUTORS

Vito Aiuto lives in New York City with his wife, Monique. They perform as The Welcome Wagon (Asthmatic Kitty Records). His first book of poems is *Self-Portrait as Jerry Quarry* (New Issues Press, 2002).

James Armstrong is the author of *Blue Lash* (Milkweed Editions, 2006) and *Monument in a Summer Hat* (New Issues Press, 2000). His poetry has appeared in various journals. He currently teaches English and creative writing at Winona State University in Winona, Minnesota.

Andrea Avery was born and raised in Rockville, Maryland. She earned her BA in music and her MFA in creative writing from Arizona State University. She lives in Phoenix with her husband and works as an editor for McMurry, Inc.

Neil Azevedo is a poet and graduate of the University of Nebraska at Omaha's Writer's Workshop, after which he went on for an MFA at Columbia University. He is editor-in-chief of Zoo Press. His first book *Ocean* was published by Grove/Atlantic in 2005.

Angela Ball's most recent book of poetry is *The Museum of the Revolution*, a long poem on Cuba. She lives in Hattiesburg, Mississippi with her dog, Maggie, and her cat, Frank O'Hara, and teaches in the University of Southern Mississippi's Center for Writers.

Claire Bateman is the author of four collections of poetry: *The Bicycle Slow Race* (1991); *Friction* (1998); *At the Funeral of the Ether* (1998); and *Clumsy* (2003). Her book *Leap* is forthcoming from New Issues Press. She teaches at the Fine Arts Center in Greenville, South Carolina.

Joshua Beckman is the author of four books of poetry, most recently *Your Time Has Come* (Verse Press, 2004). He lives in Staten Island, New York.

Bruce Bond's most recent collections of poetry include *Cinder* (Etruscan Press), *The Throats of Narcissus* (University of Arkansas) and *Radiography* (BOA). Presently he is Professor of English at the University of North Texas and Poetry Editor for *American Literary Review*.

Kevin Boyle is the author of the chapbook *The Lullaby of History*, which won the Mary Belle Campbell Poetry Book Prize, and *A Home for Wayward Girls*, which won the New Issues Poetry Prize, and was published in 2005. He works at Elon University and lives in Burlington, North Carolina.

Brigitte Byrd's first book of poetry *Fence Above the Sea* was published by Ahsahta Press in 2005. Her work has appeared or is forthcoming in *ACM, Indiana Review, New Orleans Review, The Spoon River Poetry Review, New American Writing, HOW2, Phoebe* and other places.

Victoria Chang's first book, *Circle*, won the *Crab Orchard Review* Award Series in Poetry and was published by Southern Illinois University Press in 2005. She also edited *Asian American Poetry: The Next Generation* (University of Illinois Press, 2004). She resides in Southern California.

Meghan Cleary is the author of *The Perfect Fit: What Your Shoes Say About You* from Chronicle Books. For five years she ran the poetry reading series Readings Between A and B in New York's East Village. Her poems have appeared in *The Hat, La Petite Zine*, and *Slipstream*. Visit her website at www.missmeghan.com.

Cynie Cory is the author of *American Girl* (New Issues, 2004)—a Brenda Hillman selection. Her second manuscript, *Clink Street*, was runner-up in the 2003 T.S. Eliot Poetry Prize. *Capitalist Down* is Cory's most recently completed manuscript. She teaches poetry and playwrighting at South Carolina Governor's School for the Arts & Humanities.

Denise Duhamel's most recent books are *Two and Two* (University of Pittsburgh Press, 2005), *Mille et un Sentiments* (Firewheel, 2005), and *Queen for a Day: Selected and New Poems* (University of Pittsburgh Press, 2001).

Kristy Eldredge writes about rock and roll for gloriousnoise.com and plays regularly at New York open mics, so her success is hardly to be measured on human scale.

Sybil Pittman Estess is the author of most recently *Blue, Candled in January Sun* (poetry). Her other books are *Seeing the Desert Green* (poetry), *Elizabeth Bishop and Her Art* (collected criticism), and *In a Field of Words* (creative writing textbook).

Lisa Fishman is the author of the poetry collections *The Deep Heart's Core is a Suitcase* and *Dear, Read*. A graduate of Utah's PhD program, Fishman teaches at Beloit College. Her most recent work has appeared in literary journals such as *Colorado Review*, *Indiana Review*, *Crazyhorse*, *Beloit Poetry Journal*, *Elixir*, *Poetry Salzburg Review*, and *Louisiana Literature*.

Sarah Fox lives in Minneapolis where she works as a doula, a teacher of poetry, an Americorps volunteer with Headstart, and as editor of Fuori Editions. Her book *Because Why* is forthcoming from Coffee House Press.

Mary Gannon is the editor of *Poets & Writers Magazine*. Her poems have appeared most recently in *32 Poems* and the *Paris Review*. She lives in Brooklyn, New York.

Jamey Genna received her Masters in Writing from the University of San Francisco and is a teacher in the bay area. Her work has most recently appeared in *Phantasmagoria, Georgetown Review* and *Colere*.

Matthew Guenette has worked as a landscaper, busboy, and data entry clerk. He received his MFA from Southern Illinois University, and currently lives in Bloomington, Illinois.

Anne Guzzardi lives in Nashville, Tennessee.

Julie Hensley lives and teaches in Oklahoma with her husband, the writer R. Dean Johnson. She is currently circulating *Landfall*, a novel in stories of which "Floating" is a part, and she is working on another novel. Fiction from her first cycle has recently appeared in *Fourteen Hills, Western Humanities Review, Phoebe, Redivider*, and many other journals.

David Hernandez is the author of *A House Waiting for Music*, published by Tupelo Press in 2003, and *Always Danger*, out from Southern Illinois University Press in 2006. His poems have appeared in *Southern Review, TriQuarterly, Iowa Review, Epoch, Indiana Review, AGNI*, and *Mississippi Review*. David is married to writer Lisa Glatt. Visit his website at www.DavidAHernandez.com.

Bob Hicok is shorter now than when he started writing this sentence.

Amy Holman's collection, *Wait for Me, I'm Gone*, won the 2004 Annual Dream Horse Press National Chapbook competition published in 2005. She is writing a novel, an excerpt of which appeared in the first issue of *Shade*, and is working on a writer's guide to colonies, programs and grants to be published by Perigree in 2006.

Steven Huff is the author of a book of poems, *The Water We Came From* (Foothills, 2003). He teaches creative writing at Rochester Institute of Technology, works at Seymour Library in Brockport, NY, and has a twice-weekly radio spot, "Fiction in Shorts," on NPR-affiliate station WXXI-FM.

Austin Hummell's books are *The Fugitive Kind* (University of Georgia Press), and *Poppy*, winner of the 2003 Del Sol Press Poetry Prize. He teaches at Northern Michigan University and is poetry editor of *Passages North*.

George Kalamaras is the author of *Even the Java Sparrows Call Your Hair* (Quale Press, 2004), *Borders My Bent Toward* (Pavement Saw Press, 2003), and *The Theory and Function of Mangoes* (Four Way Books, 2000), which won the Four Way Books Intro Award. Professor of English at Indiana University-Purdue University Fort Wayne, Kalamaras is the recipient of creative writing fellowships from the National Endowment for the Arts (1993) and the Indiana Arts Commission (2001). During 1994 he spent several months in India on an Indo-U.S. Advanced Research Fellowship from the Fulbright Foundation and the Indo-U.S. Subcommission on Education and Culture.

Meg Kearney is the author of *An Unkindness of Ravens* (BOA Editions, 2001) and *The Secret of Me* (Persea Books, 2005). She has taught poetry at the New School University, and is the director of the Solstice Creative Writing Programs of Pine Manor College in Massachusetts. She was the associate director of the National Book Foundation, sponsor of the National Book Awards, for more than ten years.

Ann Keniston's first collection *The Caution of Human Gestures* was published in 2005 by WordTech Communications/David Robert Books. Her poems have recently appeared in *Michigan Quarterly Review, North American Review,* and elsewhere. She teaches at the University of Nevada-Reno and lives in Reno with her husband and sons.

David Kirby is the Robert O. Lawton Distinguished Professor of English at Florida State University and the author most recently of *The Ha-Ha;* for more information, see www.davidkirby.com.

Noelle Kocot-Tomblin is the author of *4* and *The Raving Fortune* out from Four Way Books. She lives in Brooklyn, New York.

Steve Langan is the author of *Freezing* (New Issues, 2001) and *Notes on Exile & Other Poems,* which received the 2004 Weldon Kees Award from The Backwaters Press. His poems are in recent issues of *Verse, Fence, The Iowa Review, Prairie Schooner* and *Hotel Amerika.* He lives in Omaha.

Kevin Larimer is the senior editor of *Poets & Writers Magazine.* His poems have appeared most recently in *The Canary, Octopus Magazine,* and the 20th anniversary issue of *Verse.* He lives in Brooklyn.

Adrienne Lewis is the publisher/creator of The Rooftop chaplet series. She has authored two previous chapbooks of poetry: *Coming Clean (Mayapple Press)* and *Compared to This* (Finishing Line Press). Lewis has also had work published in numerous print and online literary venues. She currently teaches English at Kirtland Community College in Roscommon, Michigan and serves as the poetry editor for both the school's national literary journal *Controlled Burn* and her own zine *Paradidomi.* A chapbook of her prose titled *Past Perfect Pretense* is forthcoming from Sunnyoutside.

Beth Martinelli has taught literature and writing at Saint Vincent College, Slippery Rock University, Western Michigan University and the University of Maryland. Her poems have appeared in *Pleiades, Sonora Review, Bellingham Review, Barrow Street* and numerous other journals.

Charlotte Matthews is the author of a chapbook, *A Kind of Devotion* (Palanquin Press, 2004). Her poems have recently appeared in *Virginia Quarterly Review, Tar River, The Mississippi Review,* and *Meridian.*

K. (Kevin) A. McGowan's first book, *Rubric,* was published in 2004 by Pudding House Publications, and his second book, *No Passengers,* appeared in 2005 from The Backwaters Press. Raised in Scranton, Pennsylvania, he teaches at Remington College in Lafayette, Louisiana.

Leonard Nathan is the author of nine volumes of poetry, most recently, *Restarting the World,* out from Orchises Press in 2006. Nathan has also critiqued and translated the work of several poets. He was nominated for the National Book Award, and received the National Institutes of Arts and Letters prize for poetry, a Guggenheim, and many other awards and honors. He lives in Kensington, California.

Collier Nogues grew up in Texas and Japan, earned her B.A. from Barnard College in New York, and attends the MFA Program in Poetry at UC Irvine while living part-time in Austin. She likes to travel.

Kurt S. Olsson has published poems in the past year in *Alaska Quarterly Review, FIELD, Black Warrior Review, Quarterly West,* and elsewhere. He also has a chapbook to his credit, *I Know Your Heart, Hieronymus Bosch* (Portlandia Group).

Steve Orlen teaches at the University of Arizona and in the low-residency MFA program at Warren Wilson College. His most recent book is *This Particular Eternity,* from Ausable Press.

Ethan Paquin's third book, *The Violence,* was published in 2005 by Ahsahta Press.

Derek Pollard is currently an instructor at Lakewood Prep School in Howell, NJ. He has poems and reviews appearing or forthcoming in *Ambit* (UK*), Barrow Street, Caketrain, Columbia: A Journal of Literature and Art, Colorado Review, Diagram, Hawai'i Review, Pleiades, Poet Lore* and *Quarterly West.*

Stella Vinitchi Radulescu was born in Romania. She has a PhD in French from University of Bucharest and an MA in French from the University of Illinois at Chicago, and she is a lecturer in French at Northwestern University. Her most recent chapbook, *Self Portrait in Blue*, was published by March Street Press in 2004.

Dana Roeser's first book of poems, *Beautiful Motion*, was published in 2004 by Northeastern University Press as winner of the Samuel French Morse Prize. In 2005, Roeser won the Great Lakes Colleges Association New Writers Award and the Jenny McKean Moore Writer-in-Washington Fellowship at George Washington University. New work is forthcoming in the *Northwest Review* and *Notre Dame Review*.

Alane Rollings attended Bryn Mawr College and the University of Chicago. Her most recent poetry collections are *To Be in This Number* (TriQuarterly, 2005) and *The Logic of Opposites* (Northwestern University Press, 1998). Rollings lives in Hyde Park and teaches at the University of Chicago.

Margot Schilpp is the author of *The World's Last Night* (2001) and *Laws of My Nature* (2005); both published by Carnegie Mellon University Press. She lives in New Haven, Connecticut.

Born and raised in Connecticut, Joanna Solfrian holds a BA from Trinity College and a MFA from the University of Southern Maine's Stonecoast program. Currently, she lives in Brooklyn where she works with teenagers at a learning center. She has published poems in various journals.

Virgil Suárez was born in Havana, Cuba, in 1962. He has lived in the United States since 1974. He is the author of more than twenty books of prose and poetry. Most recently he published *90 Miles: Selected and New Poems* with the University of Pittsburgh Press. Currently he is at work on a new collection of stories, a novel, and a new book of poems. He teaches in the Low Residency MFA program at Bennington College and lives in Florida.

Elaine Terranova's most recent book of poems is *The Dog's Heart* (Orchises Press, 2002). She has new work in *Tiferet* and *Spectaculum*.

Chase Twichell's new book of poems, *Dog Language,* was published by Copper Canyon in 2005. She is the editor of Ausable Press.

Sarah Vap is an MFA candidate in poetry at Arizona State University where she is co-poetry editor for *Hayden's Ferry Review.* She has won many awards for her publications, including the Katherine C. Turner Award from the Academy of American Poets in 2003. She was also the invited poet at the 2003 Lithuania Spring Poetry Festival.

Kary Wayson is a recipient of the 2003 "Discovery" / *The Nation* award and a 2001 Artist Trust / Washington State Arts Commission Fellowship. Her poems have appeared in *Poetry Northwest, The Nation,* and *FIELD,* among others. Her chapbook, *Dog & Me,* was published in April 2004 by LitRag Press.

Joe Wenderoth grew up near Baltimore. Wesleyan University Press has published his first two books of poems: *Disfortune* (1995), and *It Is If I Speak* (2000). Shortline Editions published a chapbook, *The Endearment* (1999), and Verse Press published *Letters to Wendy's* (2000). He has two books forthcoming from Verse Press: *The Holy Spirit of Life: Texts Constructed for John Ashcroft's Secret Self,* and *Agony: A Proposal* (non-fiction). He is Associate Professor English at the University of California, Davis, where he lives with his wife and daughter.

Jennifer Willoughby is a freelance web writer and poet who lives in Minneapolis. Her work has appeared most recently in *Prairie Schooner, Rhino* and *Hayden's Ferry Review.*

Jim Zola works as a children's librarian and toy designer in Greensboro, North Carolina. He has a chapbook published by Blue Pitcher Press—*One Hundred Bones of Weather*—and a poetry manuscript in the works, titled *Between the Invisible Landscapes.*

ACKNOWLEDGMENTS:

Joshua Beckman's poems are from his series titled "Let the People Die."

Sybil Estess's poems "View of the Twin Towers from Bleecker Street in the Village, 1974" and "Scars" first appeared in *Blue, Candled in January Sun* (WordTech Communications, 2005).

Ann Keniston's poems "Anniversary," "Second Language," and "Simile" first appeared in *The Caution of Human Gestures* (WordTech Communications/David Robert Books, 2005).

Kevin McGowan's poems "No Passengers," "Sometimes We Get So Close," and "Tracks in the Water" first appeared in *No Passengers* (The Backwaters Press, 2005).

Leonard Nathan's poems "Getting Serious," "Confession," and "Winter Retrospect at the Café Solo" are reprinted from *Restarting the World* (Orchises Press, 2006) by permission of Leonard Nathan and Orchises Press.

Ethan Paquin's poem "Problem, Explained, Answered" first appeared in *Accumulus* (Salt, 2003); "Rustic II" first appeared in *The Violence* (Ahsahta Press, 2005).

David Dodd Lee is the author of four books of poems, including *Arrow Pointing North* (2002) and *Abrupt Rural* (2004). He teaches fiction and poetry at Indiana University South Bend.